More Rattling in the Closet

Yet More History of the Noble Beauderriere Family

Roger Povey

To Tom
Thank you for your support in my literary endeavours

R...

Copyright © Roger Povey 2014 All rights reserved. No part of this publication may be reproduced, stored in a retrieval system, or transmitted in any means, electronic, mechanical, photocopying. Recording or otherwise, without the prior written permission of the publisher.

ISBN: 978-1-499-51064-5

DEDICATION

This book is dedicated to the Beauderriere Family. Were it not for their little foibles and utter idiocy this book could not have been written. You may ask, did they ever exist, I answer, if they had existed then this world would have been a different place, not necessarily a better place, but different.

This book contains all of the content of my previous book 'Rattling in the Closet' but now with Authors Comments and more on the Beauderrieres. A lot of the Beauderriere papers showed their involvement with literature.

I have scoured these papers and found that many authors had incorporated a Beauderriere with in their own writings only to discard the section later.

I have also included a section on the rather stranger of the Beauderrieres, yes, stranger, unbelievable isn't it

The Beauderriere's blind and mindless skittering advance through history must have raised many an eyebrow and skirt. Anyway, what I am saying is read this book, it's funny and don't try and analyse it, I know I didn't.

A SELECTION FIRST EDITION TESTIMONIALS AND COMMENTS

A rattling good pound's worth!
This review is from: Rattling in the Closet: (Kindle)
I was planning to buy the Kindle version of War and Peace, but my brain performed a peculiar forty-five degree turn to the left, and I found myself downloading Rattling in the Closet instead. I wasn't at all disappointed, even though "Rattling" doesn't cover that particular period of Russian history, or does it? What it does cover, is a broad sweep of history from Neolithic times to the modern era, describing key events, as perverted by the bungling Beauderriere Family. This book should be required reading for all students of history, although I'm not sure that their tutors would approve. A rattling good read from start to finish. I do hope Mr. Povey has more of this in the pipeline – I'll be the first in the queue with my pound. **Amander**

Hahahahahaha,
This review is from: Rattling in the Closet (Paperback)
I so wish History was taught to me in this way at school!...I would have learned and remembered so much more stuff. I sometimes wondered if I may be distantly related to the Beauderriere family, especially the Idlebastardii.... I laughed so much...a tear ran down my leg! Fabulous read. **Miss Fishy**

45 Degree Turn To Funny,
This review is from: Rattling in the Closet (Kindle)
Roger's rewrite of history takes you on a sometimes hilarious ride through the Beauderriere's impact on the events that have shaped our world. From the Stone Age to the 20th century the bumbling antic of this Family will make you laugh and groan. **Steve Saxon**

Chapter One
My First Tentative Steps

Will we, after we are gone, make some small mark on the pages of history? It is comforting to think that we might. Most people are not able to do this, mainly because they are insignificant little nothings who would have about the same impact on history as a fart in a thunderstorm.

Others do make their mark, mainly because they are insignificant little nothings who, by quirks of fate or perhaps by sheer determination, fart louder than everyone else and have no concept of just how loud thunderstorms can be.

This leads me, inevitably, to the Beauderriere dynasty: a family that *did* have an impact, and quite an impact it was. It seems they had a hand in every major historical event.

In order to write this biography I needed advice. After much concentrated and in-depth research, with the aid of a Yellow Pages and a pin, I chose to approach a Professor Throgmorton, then living in Hastings. I had heard it said that he was an eccentric, and also an authority on the Beauderrieres. I motored down from my London address to the Sussex coast the following day.

The professor's housekeeper, Mrs Smear, showed me into a small dark room. I sat, as instructed, on a box and waited. Eventually the door flew open and I saw Mrs Smear being berated by an odd-looking man attired (as perhaps one would expect of an eccentric) in a cheap dressing gown, green Wellington boots and a deerstalker.

"Mrs Smear," said the professor, "you must make an appointment to have your eyes tested. This is the third time this month you have shown a visitor into the hall cupboard."

I was helped out of the closet. Mrs Smear gestured for me to follow the man into his study. He sat down behind his desk and offered me the chair opposite.

"Well young man," he said, "you must think we are all mad, but we're not, we are not *all* mad." He picked up an old briar pipe and filled it with what I immediately deduced to be grass clippings.

"Of course, Mrs Smear is mad, mad as a... a..."

"Hatter?" I suggested.

The professor looked at me querulously. Then he angered.

"Hate her? Of course I don't hate her," he said, "she's mad, I grant you, but you can't go about the place hating people just because they're different from one."

The difference between the professor and his housekeeper was minimal. I began to regret coming to see him. Perhaps I would forget about the Beauderrieres and find something else to fill my achingly lonely life.

"So, you want me to help you," said the professor, suddenly calmer. "You're looking into the Beauderrieres, am I right?" I was taken aback by his sudden spell of sanity. He took out a gold watch and began to wind it up.

"I got this from my father, you know," he said. "Inheritance?" I asked. He shook his head. "No, theft. I stole it from him on his death bed."

He began to swing the fob to and fro. "Your best bet," he began, "is to have a look at the ancestral home - Tanners Hall in Wiltshire."

After some searching, I found the family house. It looked its age. The grounds were overgrown and ivy smothered the walls. I stopped my car in the weed-covered drive and approached. I pushed the door open; it fell with a crash to the floor sending up a cloud of ancient dust. I entered the hallway.

In its day, it would have been a magnificent edifice. The place had been stripped and cobwebs clung to every corner. I made my way through the downstairs rooms. The walls could have told many a story. Standing to one side of the staircase was a vast brass gong; I took up the stick and struck it. The sound reverberated through the house and all manner of birds and animals squeaked and squawked.

I soon became aware of a steady footfall. It seemed to be coming from below me. I had heard many a tale of the house and its ghosts. I did not move. To my right an old oak door slowly creaked open. Soon an apparition was standing before me; old, bent and covered with cobwebs. I made the sign of the cross and screamed at the wraith:

"Go back to the depths of hell!" The spectre raised its bony arm.

"It's Monday," the phantom professed, "I always do the windows of a Monday." I asked the spirit who he was.

"Spurt, the old family container," he replied.

"You mean *retainer*," I countered.

"Whatever," said the ghoul, "you still get pissed on from a great height by the pissing aristos."

He walked over to a pane-less window and began, like a mime artist, to clean.

"There's no glass in the windows," I said, helpfully. He turned on me.

"I KNOW!, I'm not pissing mad, but it's Monday, I always do the windows of a Monday." I asked Spurt if I could look around the house.

"Do what you want, I've got work to do!" he mumbled.

I made my way tentatively up the grand stairway and wandered through the rooms. Lonely places - once they would have been full of life. I reached the top, the roof area.

As I walked the dusty attics of Tanners Hall, I came across what appeared to be a false wall. I looked around the room and found a hammer. I gave the wall a gentle tap; it came down in a flurry of lath and plaster. To my amazement the little alcove I had discovered was full of trunks, packing cases and tea chests.

Two hours later, I had prized all the containers open. Each of them was empty. I left the alcove, made my way across the attic, and saw a large portmanteau in the middle of the floor with a label that read:

Herein are the letters and other such materials of Lord Beauderriere. Pray do not break down the false wall as I store empty crates and chests in there and it cost a bloody lot of money to have it built.

I looked about furtively and opened the chest. It was full of letters, papers and documents. For the next four hours, I collected only those documents that I believed would have been of interest and left the rest, for the time being at least, to moulder with the house.

I came back down and found Spurt in the kitchen. After some encouragement, Spurt told me of the last moments of the last incumbent of the house:

It was on April 1st 1977 that the last Lord Beauderriere popped his clogs. It was rather a silly thing to do, a 90-year-old man wearing clogs I ask you. He died after a headlong fall down the grand staircase. He had been hurrying down to the front of the house; he had seen the postman cycling up the drive. He was expecting a letter from his solicitor regarding one the many litigations in which he was involved.

Lord Beauderriere's body hit the bottom of the stairs, slid across the highly polished oak floor, and came to rest next to the massive front door.

The postman put the mail through the letterbox, envelopes and a few unsolicited pieces of junk mail cascaded down on his Lordship, he looked through them. "Bugger it," he exclaimed.

Those were the last words he ever spoke. His April choice from the Encyclopedia of the Month Club struck him squarely on the head, killing him outright. His death meant an end to the long line of Lords Beauderriere who could trace their family back as far as… well, whenever it was that history was foggy or hazy… you know… the mists of time.

The late Lord Beauderriere was descended from the lineage of Charlemagne's less well-known brother Pepin the Confused. This forebear did nothing to make a dent in history, but his one and only talent was to serve the dynasty well. He was a serial shagger; it is entirely down to him that so many different branches of the family existed.

Alas, we shall never see their like again, never again will an intrepid Beauderriere, set out on an expedition, no more will a Beauderriere lead his men into battle. It is the end of an amazing line of men, women, and others. Unless, of course, somewhere out there is another Beauderriere. I hope to all that is holy that there isn't.

This book is an account gleaned from those very documents. History, as we know it, may not be correct. Many characters believed to be fictitious or the stuff of legend might actually have existed. Historians might poo-poo these documents and my interpretation of them – if indeed historians actually say 'poo'.

Beauderriere's papers covered the whole of English history; some reports come from a time before writing was introduced to, that is how special they are. Just think of it, a written history before writing was invented. Makes you think, doesn't it?

I felt I owed it to the Beauderriere family and to my dwindling bank balance to publish a book based (loosely) on what I had discovered in Lord Beauderriere's trunk. It was only after close examination of the memoirs that I discovered the awful truth, and realised that if it *were* all true (it was certainly awful) the whole of history would have to be re-written.

<u>AUTHORS NOTES ON THIS CHAPTER</u>*I knew, from the beginning that this would be an arduous task. I would be taking on established historians who would do their utmost to discredit me. But I was adamant to start this adventure and at no time was I going attempt to rewrite history. It is at this point I would like to thank Prof. Throgmorton of Hastings for his invaluable help in my search for the*

Beauderrieres. I would also like to mention that after I left his house I found that my wallet was missing and that several hundreds of pounds had been charged to my credit card. I am not casting aspersions at the illustrious professor; I would just like to say that if my wallet is returned I will take no further action.

Chapter Two
Get Off Of My Land

As we look back through the mists of time when tribes of nomadic tribesmen, were wandering... nomadically through the giant forests, we come across ancestors of the Beauderrieres. The tribe is called the Idlebastardii. It seems they decided to settle down and stop wandering.

After a few days, they are hungry and thirsty and one of the tribesmen, Grogg the Clever, turned to the chieftain, Thicke the Not-So-Clever.

"I say, O Great Leader." The rest of the tribe were in awe of Grogg, mainly they admired the way he could talk to Thicke and call him 'Great Leader' without laughing himself silly. He went on.

"I believe, O Great One, that the reason we are hungry and thirsty is due to the abrupt change in our lifestyle from hunter-gatherers to sitter-downerers doing sod all!"

Thicke pondered this for a moment and then stood up and faced his tribe.

"Friends, Nomads, the gods have spoken to me and have decreed that the reason we are hungry and thirsty is because we have changed rather too..."

"Abruptly," said Grogg quietly.

"Abruptly, yes, from hunter-gatherers to um"

"A Latin-American Formation Dance Team," said Grogg.

"To a Latin...what? Thicke looked at Grogg bewildered. Grogg stood up.

"What our Great and Wonderful Leader is saying," began Grogg, "is that we must become, er, what shall we call ourselves, Farmers, that seems a good word for it. We must clear this ground and till the soil, plant the seeds and tend them and when they are ripe, we must harvest and store them."

A man, Twitt the Argumentative, piped up from the back.

"Sounds like a lot of bloody hard work to me, why don't we go back to hunting and gathering. Maybe we don't want to become…Framers?"

"Farmers! It will be a lot of hard work," said Grogg. "But it will be worth it in the end, no longer will we have to live hand to mouth, we will be a community, we can build ourselves houses and raise animals and live in peace, what could be better than that." Twitt piped up again. "Hunting and bloody gathering."

After a little more debate and the strange death of Twitt the Argumentative, the tribe began to prepare the ground.

The years pass and we find them in the village of Thicket. The chieftain called a meeting and informed the villagers that they must raise a great monument near his house.

Sycophant the Druid stood up and said that Thicke was right; they must raise an edifice to the gods, to thank them for their munificence. Thicke agreed, but his idea for a monument was not really for the gods.

"We must build a structure of stone, a large structure, big enough for us all," said Thicke, "somewhere we can talk and relax by the light of the moon. We can put tables and seats and all sorts of things in there."

Gitt the Quarrelsome, a cousin of Twitt the Argumentative, spoke up.

"Why can't we make it out of wood? We've got stacks of wood; the nearest stone is miles away. Sounds like a lot of bloody hard work to me."

Grogg the Clever stood up and spoke. "It has to be made of stone, then it will last for millennia, people will look at it and wonder."

"Yes," said Gitt, "they'll wonder why these arseholes went miles to carve out and haul bloody great blocks of stone to build it when they were surrounded by stacks of wood."

After a little debate and the strange death of Gitt the Quarrelsome, the tribe prepared to go into the wilds of Wales to collect the stones.

It took years for the great monoliths to be erected. Many designs were discussed; square, oblong, triangular, what was the best configuration. All the options were looked at and the villagers decided that a circle of stones, with a stone on top was the best of them.

Twatt the Cantankerous, a cousin of Twitt the Argumentative and Gitt the Quarrelsome stood up and spoke.

"Okay, a circle of stones, I'll accept that, but why do you want to put stones on top, it sounds like a lot of bloody hard work to me."

Grogg the Clever began to sharpen his knife and he looked at Twatt.

"We want to put stones on top because we bloody want to." He threw his knife and it stuck in a tree inches from Twatt's head. "Any arguments?" Twatt shook his head.

So there we have it, Stonehenge was not a place of worship for druids or a landing platform for intergalactic flying saucers, or any other of the ideas that have been or are being bandied about.

It was, and still is, some sort of unfinished conservatory for those balmy evenings just after the Ice Age, when the Celtic chieftain would invite his friends and family around for a postprandial chat and a glass of whatever passed for wine in those days… wine probably.

It is fantastic to think, that all of those centuries or even millennia ago, some bright spark had the idea of adding to ones property to enhance its value on the market.

When you consider that if you wanted a house in those days, you just had to collect a few sticks and some cow dung and you could have your own beautiful home with all the comforts of the era in which you lived, plague, marauding robbers and the constant smell of cow shit.

It never occurred to the locals that this was a conservatory because it needed to be glazed and glass was not readily available in this area so it was really a waste of time.
The builders picked up their tools and wandered slowly off into the mists of time leaving us with the mystery that has haunted us for all time, until now that is!

AUTHORS NOTES ON THIS CHAPTER
I am aware that the above is all conjecture and that you think I probably made it up. I have used historical records and an understanding of Beauderriere attitudes to put together a scenario that could have possibly perhaps occurred. I am not saying that it did, but I am saying if it did, it would have happened exactly like I have written.

Chapter Three
I Came, I Saw I Pissed Off Again

As we totter a little forward in history, we come across Scabies, another of the Beauderriere's ancestors. Scabies was a chieftain whose tribe inhabited a region of the South Coast of England; they didn't know it was England at that time. Scabies called it Scabialand.

As Scabies and his tribe were idly wandering around the cliff edge, they saw a fleet of boats heading towards them. Scabies turned to Dysenteric, his brother.

"What do you make of that?" he said.

"Tourists, nothing to worry about," said Dysenteric.

"What do you mean, tourists, they look like invaders," said Scabies.

"Who in their right mind," said Dysenteric, "would want to invade this septic isle, this gallstone set in a shivery sea?" Scabies pondered for a moment and then leapt into action.

"Time for dinner, I think," he said.

As the tribe sat down to eat, Dysenteric looked at the boats out at sea. "They're getting nearer; I think we should prepare to meet them."

In the leading boat stood a man, resplendent in armour. This was Julius Caesar, one of Rome's greatest men. He looked every inch a fighting man. He turned to a soldier standing next to him.

"What's this place called, Lucius?" he asked.

"It's not on the map, Great Caesar," Lucius replied.

"Okay, we will invade and add this land to the might that is Rome," said Caesar.

"It may belong to someone else, Caesar."

"It's mine now, okay?"

The fleet arrived at the beach and the Romans disembarked. They lined themselves up and Caesar surveyed his new acquisition. The following conversation has been freely translated from Latin:

"What are you going to call this place, eh, Julius?"

"I don't know, Lucius, maybe Juliusland, or Caesarland, I'm not sure yet."

Lucius took Caesar by the arm; they walked for a few yards.

"Julius, I don't want the men to hear this, but you're getting a lot of bad press back home, you've got stop naming everywhere after yourself, certain members of the Senate are starting to talk, they think you're trying to take over."

"Okay, okay, Lucius, we'll call it North Land Albion, because of those white cliffs."

"North Land Albion," said Lucius, "it sounds like a football team!"

"You name it then!" said Caesar in a huff.

"How about, Albion, it's got a nice ring to it."

"Okay, let's get going," Caesar ordered, he took hold of his Eagle Banner and planted into the sand.

"I claim this land for the Senate and People of Rome and I call it Albion."

Lucius looked across the sand and saw Scabies and his people walking towards them.

"Shit, we're for it now!" he whispered.

Caesar followed his gaze and turned to Lucius.

"Go and tell them, this land now belongs to Rome."

Lucius, after some persuasion walked toward Scabies and his tribe.

The following conversation can only be supposed and is based on the events that happened at that time.

"Hail, I am Lucius Flaccidus Postcoiatal, the second in command to Gaius Julius Caesar, conqueror of the known world."

"Piss off, this is our land!" said Scabies.

"You must lay down your arms and surrender to the might that is Rome!" retorted Lucius.

"Bollocks," said Dysenteric, "we're not giving up without a fight!"

"You can never stand up to the mighty Roman army," said Lucius proudly. Scabies looked at the Romans standing on the beach.

"I see about five hundred of you," he said, "I've got five thousand at my command, look."

At the top of the cliff a long line of woad-covered men could be seen, all brandishing spears. Lucius looked at Scabies.

"One moment, I'll just have a word with Caesar."

Scabies and Dysenteric nodded and they watched Lucius walk back to Caesar and the army. An argument was in progress, there was a lot of arm waving and pacing up and down.

They heard Caesar shout 'Five thousand, bleeding hell'. Then Lucius returned.

"Right, I'm awfully sorry, but we can't stay, we've got an appointment in Gaul, we hope to return later."

"Okay," said Scabies, "perhaps another time, have a safe trip."

"Thank you," said Lucius. He returned to Caesar and the fleet quickly embarked and sailed off. Dysenteric and Scabies laughed. "Tossers, they won't be back," said Scabies.

AUTHORS NOTES ON THIS CHAPTER

Caesar was to return the next year and subdue the natives and began the 400 years of Roman subjugation. When Emperor Claudius invaded 10 years after Julius Caesar, he brought an elephant with him. I think Scabies mated with it and started the Beauderriere dynasty. Again this chapter is a slight conjecture, but it is supported by many Roman writers of the time, that mention a rough people inhabiting a precious realm beyond the clouds, and you don't get rougher than the Beauderrieres.

Chapter Four
Revenge! Revenge!

A little later, the Romans came back and defeated the islanders. This caused another scion of the Idlebastardii, Queen Beaudercia, to get her knickers in a twist. The Roman Governor, one Limpdicus Coietus Interruptus, called Beaudercia to his presence.

"May I say, at first, how terribly sorry I am to hear of your husband's death and the Emperor would also like to extend his sympathies," began Limpdicus,
"I also understand that in his will, your husband left his kingdom to both you, your daughters and the Emperor."

"Yes," said Beaudercia, "he went completely mad in the end and did that."

"Are you averse to sharing your kingdom with the Emperor?" asked Limpdicus.

"Too effing true mate," said Beaudercia, "it's all mine and I'm keeping it, you can tell Nero to piss off."

Limpdicus eyed the Queen warily; he then eyed her daughters lustfully.

"And your two, lovely, plump-breasted daughters are in agreement?"

"Yes, they are," said Beaudercia, "and nothing will change our minds."

A few days later, Beaudercia woke up from the savage beating she received and her two daughters were able to get some sleep after the continual shagging they had to undergo. The Governor and his troops stopped outside the hut of Beaudercia.

"I'm off to the other side of the country to subdue some Druids," he said, "now you be a good girl while I'm gone, and perhaps I'll bring you back something nice." He rode off laughing loudly.

Beaudercia was not a woman to take this kind of ridicule lightly. She took her daughters back to her village and concocted a plan to take her revenge.

"And then do you know what they did?" she asked her tribe.

"No," they said in unison. "What did they do?"

"They beat and whipped me, then they raped me and my sweet innocent daughters, it was horrific, but strangely erotic," she said gazing into the distance fondling her sword hilt.

Her second-in-command, Cunnilingus, looked over to her.

"They didn't rape you, just the girls; they just beat and whipped you." he said. Beaudercia turned and looked at him.

"They may have raped me when I was unconscious from the beating," she said. One of her daughters leant over to her.

"No, they didn't rape you; they said they preferred someone younger"

"Never mind that now, I was just saying.."

"More attractive..." said another daughter.

"Let's get on with..." said Beaudercia.

"Not so smelly..." said the first daughter.

"Shut up!" screamed Beaudercia, "What they did or didn't do is of no consequence, what concerns us is what we're going to do in revenge, I have a plan!"

She collected together all her warriors and headed for the nearest Roman town. As they arrived on a hill, Beaudercia looked down on the town and called her second-in-command to her side.

"Well, there they are, Cunnilingus, lying there, unsuspecting, vulnerable," said Beaudercia, "we will have no trouble with them."

"No, my queen, I think if we enter the town near the hot baths and make our way down the Via Haute Couture... "

"Hot baths, began Beaudercia," Haute Couture, what's that, Cunnilingus?"

"Well, hot baths are pools of water where you can wash and rest while slaves massage and manipulate you with fine oils and give you food and wine," said Cunnilingus.

"I see," said Beaudercia, "and Haute Couture?"

"That is where the ladies of the town go to buy fine gowns and robes made from silk and satin and furs."

"Gowns, hot baths, good food," said Beaudercia, "The Romans aren't all that bad are they? We could learn a lot from them."

So Beaudercia and her warriors threw down their weapons and made their way to the town of Londinium to enjoy the fruits of the Roman occupation.

"I'm still very annoyed with them," said Beaudercia as she chomped her way through a swan. "One day, one day, I'm going to get my revenge. Pass the salmon, will you?"

AUTHORS NOTES ON THIS CHAPTER

As we are now well aware, it was a cousin of Beaudercia, named Boudicca, who eventually went to war against the Romans.

Chapter Five
From The Wrath of The Vikings Deliver Us!

We must now plod on through the mists of time to find another Beauderriere ancestor. Many tales have been told of Vikings invading our green and pleasant land, with just the thought of rape and pillage on their pagan minds.

Far away in the chilly depths of Scandinavia, lived the family of King Sven the Bucolic - ancestors of the Beauderrieres. They lived out their lives, fishing and... well, fishing mostly. King Sven had six sons, Sven the Younger, Sven the Even-Younger, Sven the Younger-Than-The-Other-Two, Sven A Year-Younger-Than-Sven the Younger-Than-The-Other-Two, Sven the Youngest and Erik.

King Sven was called the Bucolic because of his liking for the quiet life. He was happy to farm and fish, and give his sons stupid bloody names. When the boys had grown to manhood, they decided that farming and fishing was not for them. They wanted to travel the world and see far-off lands.

They went to their father and asked him for their inheritance. All he could give them was his old longship and a collection of rusty old swords and shields.

"What can we do with these?" said one of the Sven's or Erik.

"I have no idea, perhaps you can trade them," he said.

"Trade them! Who in their right mind would give us anything for a pile of rusty armament?" said Erik or one of the Svens.

The boys took the weapons and loaded them into the longship. They spent quite a long time cleaning and polishing the weapons until they shone. Erik suddenly had an idea.

"Let's kill the miserly old sod and steal his money," he said. One of the Svens admonished him.

"He is our father and our King; we must make our own way in the world. Anyway, I've tried it before and he's too wily, the old bastard."

"Why don't we go over to England and sell them our weapons, the English are gullible. I mean, look at that conservatory they built. Out of stone! I ask you, with all that wood around," said one of the other Svens.

So it was decided, they would set up an armaments company. They wanted to take advantage of the new language and numbering fad called Latin, so they called themselves 'The VI Kings' (The Six Kings).

Soon Erik and the Svens were making their way to the English coast. They could see people on the shore. Sven the Younger stood proudly in the prow of the boat and looked at the people milling around. He firmly believed that they were going to make their fortune. He turned to his brothers.

"We don't want them to think we're invaders," he said, "we must make clear our intentions before we land."

The six brothers picked up their swords and shields and began waving them at the group on the beach and shouting.

"We're the VI Kings, you will get a good rate and make a killing with our swords and shields, we can give you a good rate for your village, but there is a price we won't go under. You'll look good to your women, you're lucky we turned up!"

The people on the beach looked out at the longship. Their leader, Swain the Know-All turned to his men.

"They look like invaders, what are they shouting?" Swain's religious advisor, and one-time lover, Brother Sextus strained his ear.

"I can't quite hear, wait a minute, oh no, they're saying, they're Vikings, whatever that is, they say they're going to kill us with their swords and rape all the women in the village and then they'll go and plunder, I think!"

Swain the Know-All called his men to get their swords and shields. They stood on the beach, waved at them, and shouted back.

"We don't want you here, we have our own weapons ready and we'll use them, we can assure your destruction, we will never surrender, you black-hearted pagans!"

Back on the boat, Sven the Younger turned to his brother, Sven... the whatever. "What are they saying?"

"I can't quite hear," said Sven the whatever, "something about having weapons or their own and not needing ours. They are insured by Black Heart Pagan Assurance or something like that."

Sven the Younger looked disappointed.

"Oh, well, we tried, let's go home and do some fishing, we're good at that."

The boat turned around and headed home. The people on the beach cheered and waved their weapons. Swain stood defiantly.

"We showed them, history will show how Swain the Know-All defended his land and repulsed an invasion of the blood-thirsty Vikings."

Swain was right, the VI Kings became corrupted to Vikings and they passed into history as unchristian devils bent on death and destruction when fact they were merely a company of itinerant sword and shield salesmen with a rather aggressive sales technique.

Other long ships went to England to sell their wares. When monks, sitting in their Scriptoriums, looked out of their windows and saw the Danish long ships with shields hanging along their sides and groups of men waving swords at them, it still did not occur to them that they were salesmen.

The Vikings gave up the armoury business when they realised that the English would pay them to go away anyway.

AUTHORS NOTES ON THIS CHAPTER

I have always believed that the Vikings were not as evil as they have been painted. As history is written by the victors, or if they can't write the losers, the Vikings have had bad press. When you are a monk, sitting alone in your room with only a spluttering taper to light your darkness, you are going to start seeing bogey men under the bed and in dark corners. If they had invited the Vikings to visit, they would have been pleasantly surprised...and killed probably.

Chapter Six
1066 et al

The Beauderrieres really came into prominence during the Industrial Revolution and it was Isambard Kingdom Beauderriere who first had the idea of building a tunnel under the English Channel. With the financial backing from his immensely wealthy family, he began the massive task.

Everything was going well until Beauderriere's old friend and nemesis, Bartholomew, the 8th Earl of Petit-Mort decided to lend a hand. Petit-Mort took over the digging and decided on a 45° turn to the right, he did not know why; it just seemed the right thing to do.
It wasn't long before the tunnel emerged on the Isle of Man, and a strange feeling came over him.

The Petit-Mort family had been close the Beauderrieres for centuries, ever since the Norman Conquest. Beauderriere, Count of Bourgeois, a wealthy landowner came over the Channel with William the Conqueror in 1066, well not literally *with* him; he actually came over a bit later.

As was normal in those far off days, knights took their serfs and retainers along to fight for their liege lord. In this case the knight was also expected to supply horses and a ship. In the past, shipwrights at the coastal ports normally built ships; this seemed the right way to go about it, what with there being water and everything.

Beauderriere found out that it would be cheaper to build the ship from wood from his own vast forests and transport the ship to the sea, rather than pay someone at the coast.

So his workers began felling trees and making planks and eventually finishing what Count Beauderriere thought was a fine craft. The work completed, Beauderriere began the monumental task of transporting the ship to the coast. After many days, they arrived at the coast only to find that William had sailed on the morning tide. It took nearly all day to load men, horses and provisions, but the Count was ready to leave on the evening tide.

The tranquility of the dock area was shattered by the arrival of Count Godfroi de Petit-Mort, brother-in-law to Beauderriere as well as his friend. Count Godfroi quite wrongly believed that he was the greatest navigator in the world and insisted that he take over the rudder. Not wanting to upset Godfroi, Beauderriere agreed and soon strong backs were rowing the ship out into the channel.

Once they were in open water, Count Beauderriere saw the white cliffs of Dover and announced that they were nearly there. Petit-Mort now insisted that he be navigator and that he tell them when they are nearly there. Smugly he made a 45° turn to port. Beauderriere watched as the coast of England faded into the distance.

After steering an erratic course, the ship was landed at an unknown stretch of coastline. They walked up the beach and Beauderriere ordered one of his knights, Sir Turiste de Troph, to go on ahead and scout the countryside. TT, as he was known, walked the whole of the thirty-seven and a half miles of the island and returned to say that he had managed to conquer the whole territory with only his men-at-arms and that England was not as big as people thought it was.

Beauderriere thought such endeavour warranted a reward, so he gave Sir Turiste a gold goblet and said it was for TT's successful race around the island.

Soon they decided to head for home, this time Petit-Mort was happy to let Beauderriere navigate. Beauderriere assumed that all he had to do was sail straight across the sea to get back to Normandy. This he did and soon sighted land. He and his army landed on the west coast of England, and believing it to be Normandy, he headed for his estates deep in the interior. After reaching what he thought was his estate, he decided to build a castle to commemorate his victory.

AUTHORS NOTES ON THIS CHAPTER

It was my assured intention of dealing with the Norman Invasion in greater depth, but then I hit on this Isle of Man TT race idea and went with that. You must allow me a little poetic license y'know.

Chapter Seven
The Virgin's Fair or Unfair

In the far off days of the Dark Ages, the village of Beauderriere was known as an area populated with an abundance of rather promiscuous young ladies and as a consequence virgins were a bit thin on the ground.

The then head of the House of Beauderriere, Sir Inglebert the Priapic, called for his Captain of the Guard, Gilbert De Procurer, to come to him.

Gilbert entered the great hall and stopped by the vast oak table that dominated the room.

"Now Gilbert," said Inglebert, "we have work to do."

"Your wish is my command, my Lord." Inglebert leant forward on the table.

"I am sure you are aware, that it will soon be time for the Virgins Fair." Gilbert grinned widely.

"Oh yes, my liege," he slavered, "a time of great feasting and carousing, with dances and singing by minstrels, plays by mummers and merry-andrews... I... "

"Yes, yes, all that," said Inglebert, but we mustn't forget the virgin shagging, must we."

"Oh, no, my liege," agreed Gilbert, "the virgin shagging is an integral part of the proceedings."

"Then to horse, Gilbert," commanded Inglebert, "scour my lands and have all the virgins brought to me in time for the fair." Gilbert gave Inglebert a sidelong look.

"All the virgins, my liege."

"Yes, search every village, every hamlet, and every lonely cottage hidden in the forest, everywhere. Bring me virgins!"

"There might be a teensy-weensy problem with that, my Lord."

"Problem, I do not see any problem, be gone!"

"I will do my very best, my liege."

Gilbert walked towards the door and Inglebert called after him.

"Don't forget... *virgins*!

"Yes, my Lord."

"With big tits, if possible!"

"Yes, my Lord."

"And arses like peaches. All round soft and..."

"Yes, my Lord, I know the prerequisites, I will not forget to get all the minstrels and mummers and..."

"Yes, yes, yes, I know, now go."

As Gilbert rode from the Hall followed by his guard, he looked worried. His sergeant, Wilikin de Darwin, rode up to him.

"You look worried, sir," he said.

"Where the hell am I going to find any virgins around here, what his Lordship hasn't had, everyone else has."

"That is a rather sticky problem, sir," said Wilikin. "What do you propose to do about it?"

"I don't know, I really don't!" said Gilbert exasperatedly.

"If I might venture a suggestion, sir?"

"Go ahead."

"We both know that virgins around these parts are like hen's teeth, non-existent or perhaps just a distant memory, because who's to say that hens didn't have teeth at one time, it's my belief that evolution has..."

"Yes, I know all about your theories, Darwin, what do you have in mind?"

"Where would you go if you wanted to guarantee you would find some virgins?"

"I don't know, Virgins R Us? If I knew that, I would be going there, wouldn't I, Darwin," sneered Gilbert.

"Well, it's obvious, sir, a nunnery!"

"A nunnery, Darwin!"

"Yes, sir, full to the rafters with virgins!"

"Darwin, that's the most disgraceful, blasphemous idea anyone has had. You are suggesting we raid a nunnery to get the virgins for the Virgins Fair!"

"But it's so obvious, sir."

"Sergeant, Darwin, Wilikin, Willy, let me tell you a story. Once upon a time, all the nunneries in this area were full to the brim with virgins, you couldn't move for them, and then one day, our liege lord, Lord Inglebert the Stiffy, Lord Inglebert the 'Is-That-A-Dagger-In-Your-Pocket-Or-Are-You-Just-Pleased-To-See-Me', one day, he appointed his brother, Aldus the Shag-Anything-That-Moves, as Bishop. Consequently virgins in nunneries around here are very rare indeed, rarer even than hen's dentures."

"I see, that is a problem," said Darwin.

As they rode on, they saw a monastery in the distance. Gilbert spurred his horse on. They entered the courtyard and dismounted. Gilbert told Darwin to feed the horses and the men. Then he strode into the cloisters calling out for the abbot.

"Father Claude, I have a task for you!" On entering the refectory he found Father Claude bent over the table with his cassock over his head.

"Your wish is my command, captain."

"No, not that Father Claude. How long will it take you and your scribes to write twenty letters that say, I, [INSERT NAME HERE], hereby affirm that I am a virgin and am willing to take part in the Beauderriere Virgin Fair."

"Well, let me see, twenty letters, twenty scribes, about four weeks, I'd say," replied Father Claude.

"I see," mused Gilbert. "And how long will it take these twenty scribes to do twenty letters saying I, [INSERT NAME HERE], hereby affirm that I am a virgin and am willing to take part in the Beauderriere Virgin Fair, when they have a dagger at their throat?"

"Oh, well, in that case, it will take about an hour," said Claude nervously.

"Good, good, that is acceptable, now I am hungry; bring on platters laden with meat, and fowl and pitchers of good wine."

"I'm sorry, sir, but we have no meat or fowl or wine, we are fasting because it is the eve of St Griswold the Obese, and we only have gruel and water."

"Gruel and water!" repeated Gilbert.

"Very nice gruel," said Claude.

"And the water..."

"Oh, it's very nice water, from our own well," encouraged Claude.

"Very nice gruel and very nice water, I see," said Gilbert. He fingered his dagger.

"So be it, bring me platters of very nice gruel and pitchers of very nice water!" Father Claude began to scurry away. "Father Claude!"

Father Claude stopped and returned to Gilbert who pulled him down by his sleeve. "And lots and lots of very nice salt!"

Soon Gilbert was ready to leave, the twenty letters secure in his saddlebag. He waved to Father Claude.

"Thank you, Father, for the meal, it was very nice!"

Gilbert led his men from the monastery and rode off on his renewed quest. Father Claude waved him goodbye.

"Goodbye, you wanker!" He turned and called to a friar.

"Brother, now those arseholes are gone, get out the meat and fowl and the wine, it's time for dinner. Oh, I assume you urinated in the gruel?"

"Oh yes, Father Abbot, we all did."

"Well done, well done."

The horsemen rode on, Gilbert was enjoying the adventure, he hadn't been out riding since last Michelmas, when he came upon a peasant in the forest and used him for target practise. Soon they came to a clearing in the forest, sitting on a stool was a beautiful young lady, and she was milking a cow.

Gilbert dismounted and walked over to her. His eyes were riveted on her slow long strokes of the cow's teats. Gilbert was mesmerised. As the milk spurted into the wooden bucket, Gilbert gave a moan of relief, covered his groin with his hat, and sat down.

"You seem to have spilt something on your tights, sir," she said.

Gilbert looked down at the spreading stain on his tights. "Oh, yes, it's gruel... er... very nice gruel," he answered.

The girl got up and holding her apron began to wipe the 'gruel' off of his tights.

"That feels better, doesn't it, sir," she cooed.

Gilbert stood up very quickly still covering his groin. He believed that if he took his hand away from the hat, it would remain there, as if on a coat peg.

"I... I have come here on business," Gilbert informed the girl. "I would like to see your father."

"So would my mother, sir, "we haven't seen him since last Michelmas!"

"I... I see, very sad, then I would like to see your mother!"

"So would I, sir, I haven't seen her since last Christmas, when she went up to the Hall to help serve the Christmas feast for his Lordship."

Gilbert's mind went back to last Christmas at the Hall when he had thrown an old peasant woman on the fire for spilling gravy down his tights pulled himself together.

"Well, it's you I've come to see, I am looking for virgins to attend the Beauderriere Virgin Fair," informed Gilbert. "Are you a virgin?"

The girl coyly blushed. "Well, of course, sir, I'm a good girl."

"Are you sure?" The girl looked at him angrily.

"Of, course I'm sure, I think I would know if somebody had deflowered me, but there again, I am a heavy sleeper." Gilbert couldn't believe what he was hearing.

"Are you telling me, that you have never indulged in fuc... sha... the pleasures of the flesh?"

"Well, I may have inadvertently masturbated while washing, but that's all, does that mean I'm not a virgin, sir?" she said, trying not to cry.

"No, no, of course not, that's okay, we all like a really good wan... er, wash now and again."

"Thank you, sir."

"Right, I will send a lady of the court to you in a week and she will bring you to the Hall, you must consider yourself a very lucky young lady, you are going to take part in the Beauderriere Virgins Fair!"

The girl waved them off. Gilbert turned to Darwin and gave him the twenty letters. "Have your men find the other girls, virgins or not, and bring them to the Hall in a week."

"But won't his Lordship realise that they are not all virgins?" queried Darwin.

"We'll get him drunk," said Gilbert, "he'll have this one first, the virgin, and all the rest will just be a blur to him."

"Well done, sir, it looks like another successful Virgins Fair is on the cards!"

"Yes," Gilbert mused. He looked at Darwin.

"Fancy a chat when we get back?" he asked.

"Why not!" said Darwin, "then I can tell you all about my theories, that's something to look forward to, isn't it?"

"Yes, Willy, I suppose so!" sighed Gilbert.

AUTHORS NOTES ON THIS CHAPTER

I don't know why I started this 'Authors Notes On This Chapter' lark. It seemed a good idea when I had something to say about the chapter, I may continue or I may not. It's my book!

Chapter Eight
You've Brought Me The Holy What?

For centuries men have sought the Holy Grail. They have risked life and limb to find it, but none have been successful, and now, unfortunately no one will, if this account of a Beauderriere ancestor can be believed.

It was Sir Ingelram de Beauderriere who took the Crusaders Cross and followed his liege lord across the world to the Holy Land. He didn't really want to go; he was quite happy singing ballads and writing poetry. It was his father, Sir Eustache, who insisted. He had sat down with his advisors to discuss the 'problem' of Ingelram.

"He's a very polite young man, Sir Eustache," said one of his advisors.

"Politeness doesn't butter any parsnips, Sir Gallifrand, no parsnips at all."

"I fully agree, sir, covering root vegetables with dairy produce is important, but he is a rather delicate youth," said Gallifrand.

"What the blazes are you going on about, root vegetables... I'm using metaphors!"

"I haven't tried metaphors, are they like a turnip?" asked Gallifrand.

"Just shut up and listen, you brainless dolt!" said Eustache. "Why shouldn't Ingelram go to the Holy Land?"

Sir Gallifrand looked at the other advisors who urged him on visually.

"Well, sir, as I have said, he is rather delicate youth, I'm not sure that the harsh desert air will suit him."

"What do you mean, delicate?" inquired Sir Eustache.

"Well," said Gallifrand, shifting uneasily in his seat. "The majority of those going to the Holy Land are rather rough, coarse soldiers and I'm not sure that Ingelram will be able to cope with that." Sir Eustache stood up and paced the room.

"What are you talking about? I have reports that Ingelram has rough coarse soldiers going in and out of his rooms day and night, what makes you think he would not be able to cope?"

"Perhaps, you're right, Sir Eustache," said Gallifrand," a few months in the Holy Land is sure to make a man of him."

"So, it is agreed, Ingelram will represent the House of Beauderriere in the Holy Land," instructed Eustache.
Sir Gallifrand and the other advisors looked at each other.

"Heaven and its Angels help us!" they said in unison.

Soon Ingelram was ready for his departure. His guards and baggage train were ready. His father stood at the top of the stone steps and called out to the assembled throng.

"This is a great day in the history of the House of Beauderriere, my son, Ingelram, is the first Beauderriere to take the Crusaders cross and travel to the Holy Land to take back the city of Jerusalem."

The crowds below cheered. Ingelram turned to his Captain of the Guards.

"What's he talking about Jerusalem for? I thought I was going on holiday to Holyhead." His father continued.

"Godspeed, my son, come back victorious," he said. "But if you should spill your blood in the land where Our Saviour walked, you will consider it fortuitous."

"No-one mentioned spilling blood," said Ingelram," what's all this about spilling blood!" Sir Eustache raised a goblet of wine.

"I drink to your safe return, my son, but if you should die on the edge of a Saracen sword, think your death worthwhile, because you died in God's work."

Ingelram was about to speak to his father when the trumpets sounded and they started their journey. After months of travelling, skirmishes, dysentery and rather a nasty spot on his upper lip, he arrived in Jerusalem.

One evening, he was called to the quarters of Sir Godfroi de Bouillabaisse, the Count de Petit-Mort, and the Commander-in-Chief of the Crusaders.

"Ah, Sir Ingelram, take a seat, have some wine," said Sir Godfroi. "I have a task for you to undertake"
Ingelram shifted uncomfortably in his seat.

"I must first swear you to secrecy" continued Sir Godfroi, "it is imperative that what I am going to show you must not be shown to anyone else," said Godfroi.

He then put his hand into his tights and pulled out a key. Ingelram sighed with relief. Sir Godfroi stood up and went over to a large chest. He opened it and returned with something covered by a gold cloth.

"What I have here, people have been searching for centuries to find." He took off the cloth and Ingelram saw that he was holding a large clay cup.

"Do you know what this is, Ingelram?" said Godfroi in a whisper.

Ingelram nodded. "Yes, it's a large clay cup!" he said.

"Of course, it's a large clay cup, you dolt!" shouted Sir Godfroi, "but it is more than that, it's... "

"It's...it's... "

"Yes, yes, go on Ingelram!" said Godfroi.

"It's your large clay cup," said Ingelram triumphantly.

Sir Godfroi looked at Sir Ingelram for a moment. He saw the wide-eyed innocence, a look of complete and utter stupidity. He was just the person he needed to undertake this quest.

"What this is, Ingelram," said Sir Godfroi reverently, "is Our Lord's Cup, the Cup He used at the Last Supper, the Cup that held His blood when He was crucified, this is... The Holy Grail!" Ingelram started at it for a moment. "Stuff me!" said Ingelram.

Sir Godfroi placed the Cup into Sir Ingelram's hands.

"Yes, my words exactly when I first saw it," said Sir Godfroi, "we found it here in Jerusalem and now we must send it to Rome where this most holy of relics could be placed in the hands of the Pope for safety and maximum profit." Sir Ingelram looked at the Cup and then a realisation came over him.

"That would be a perilous task for anyone," he said, "you would have to find someone very brave or very stupid to undertake a quest like that." He looked up and saw Sir Godfroi staring at him smiling.

"Stuff me!" said Sir Ingelram, again. Sir Godfroi sat back.

"You are the perfect one to take it, no one would suspect you were carrying it, they would just assume you were clearing off back home."

"Clearing off back home, you make me sound like a coward!" said Sir Ingelram.

"Everybody knows you'd rather not be here, you don't like fighting, so you're the obvious choice!"

"If I agree to undertake this quest, I want it to be known that I was leaving for a reason other than cowardice!" said Sir Ingelram.

Sir Godfroi stood up and paced the room. He turned to Ingelram.

"I shall tell people that you have to return to your estates because your father is unwell," said Sir Godfroi.

"Okay," said Sir Ingelram, "then I shall go to Rome to take the most precious of all objects to the Pope."

"Good man, I knew I could trust you, have a safe journey and confide in no one."

After months of travelling, skirmishes, dysentery and a rather nasty spot on his lower lip Ingelram reached the outskirts of Rome. His dismounted from his horse, took the Holy Grail from his saddlebag and placed it on the ground.

He dropped to his knees to give thanks to God for his and the relic's safe return when his heavily armoured knees crushed the Grail to dust. Ingelram was devastated.

Ingelram spent days trying, racking his brain on how to resolve this problem when a thought struck him. He drew his sword and started to cut down a tree, he took a slice one and a half inches thick and eighteen inches across and placed it in his saddlebag.

He mounted his horse and started for the city. As he went, he rehearsed his speech to the Pope.

'No, Your Holiness, we did not find the Holy Grail, the cup our Lord used at the Last Supper, but we did find the Holy Breadboard that Christ used to make the sandwiches for the feast!'

Nobody knows what the Pope thought of or did with the 'relic', but Ingelram did walk with a funny gait for some time afterwards.

AUTHORS NOTES ON THIS CHAPTER
I have really enjoyed this writing chapter.

Chapter Nine
Bring me Some Sharpened Steaks

One of the Beauderriere forebears fought at Agincourt with King Henry V, it wasn't too long before the king got tired of continually fighting with him and sent him home.

It wasn't for just this reason; mainly it was because the King had asked Beauderriere to arrange for a row of sharpened stakes to be placed in front of his archers.

Bewildered as usual, Beauderriere went off, and soon came to a farm. He walked up to the door and knocked.

"Open up in the name of the King!" he exhorted.

"What King?" came a reply from inside the farmhouse.

"The true and rightful King of France!" replied Beauderriere.

"Oh, you mean, King Charles the Sixth of France," said the farmer.

"Who?" queried Beauderriere.

"You don't sound very French to me, whoever you are!" replied the farmer.

"I'm not French," said Beauderriere, "I am Marauder, Lord Beauderriere, the representative of the true King of France, King Henry the Fifth of England…and France."

"Beauderriere, that's a joke isn't it?" said the farmer.

"What do you mean a joke?"

"Well," said the farmer, "it means 'lovely arse', I mean, it's a joke!" Beauderriere looked around at his men who were giggling quietly.

"It is a name I proudly bear, now, OPEN THIS BLEEDING DOOR!" he screamed. The door slowly opened to reveal an old man with white hair and beard.

"What do you want?" the farmer enquired.

"I have been ordered, by my King…" began Beauderriere.

"King Henry the Fifth…" said the farmer.

"Yes…"

"Not Charles the Sixth…"

"No… he has ordered me to collect some steaks," said Beauderriere, "so you must let me have your cattle."

What do you want with them?" asked the farmer.

"I want you to slaughter and butcher them and then cut up the steaks," demanded Beauderriere.

"Why do you want to do that?" asked the farmer.

"Because my King has demanded it!" said Beauderriere.

"My King hasn't, why should I do it for your King?" said the farmer.

"Because he is also the King of Fra… I don't want to go through that again!" said Beauderriere. He marched to the back of the farmhouse and set his men slaughtering the animals.

It wasn't long before Beauderriere had a pile of steaks in front of him.

"Right men, sharpen them," he ordered.

Soon he was riding back to the King. He had the newly sharpened steaks piled high on a platter. He stood in front of King Henry.

"What the hell are those?" asked Henry angrily.

"The sharpened steaks you requested, my liege."

The King paced up and down his tent. He turned to Beauderriere. "I have another task for you." the King said.

"Beauderriere, I need you to go back to England and bloody well stay there!"

AUTHORS NOTES ON THIS CHAPTER

Yes, I know, stupid joke, but it adds another chapter to the book.

Chapter Ten
Right, Now Make A Left Turn

Many of the Beauderrieres were sons of the sea. Septimus Beauderriere had no intention to go to America. He had no idea where or what America was. He wasn't an ignorant man; nobody had heard of it, it hadn't been discovered yet.

He was a friend of Columbus. He had to listen to the ramblings of his friend, night after night.

"Do you know what I'm going to do, Septimus?" Columbus would begin.

"Don't tell me, let me guess, um… discover a way westward to China and make a lot of money!" said Beauderriere.

"Yes," said Columbus, "sail across to the other side of the Atlantic Ocean, no-one's ever done it before!"

"St Brendan did!" said Beauderriere.

"No-one," said Columbus.

"Erik the Red did!" said Beauderriere.

"Not a soul has ever done it!" said Columbus.

"Whatever, when are you going to do this then?" asked Beauderriere. Columbus became pensive.

"I need to raise money, to purchase ships and then round up a few good sailors to crew them."

"Where are you going to get money from, you're penniless and destitute, and I'm poorer than you?" asked Beauderriere.

"I will beg an audience with the King and Queen of Spain," said Columbus, "they will support me."

"Okay," said Beauderriere, "you get the money, I'll get the sailors."

The two men parted and went their separate ways, Columbus to the Royal Palace and Beauderriere to several dockside inns. We will follow Beauderriere, because we know that the King and Queen of Spain coughed up the money.

Beauderriere stood outside of the 'Galloping Pox'; he opened the door and entered. He looked around the squalid den of iniquity.

"I say, me hearties, I need some sailors!" bawled Beauderriere.

All the occupants of the inn dropped their trousers and bent over tables.

"No, not for that...at the moment," said Beauderriere eyeing them, "for something else!" The men pulled up their trousers and sat down.

"What for?" said a grizzled old sea dog.

"For adventure!" cried Beauderriere.

"Piss off!" said the grizzled old sea dog.

"Piss off, you wanker!" said all of the occupants of the inn. Beauderriere thought for a moment.

"Adventure...and plunder, and oriental ladies!" he said.

One sailor, bedecked in a floral shirt that had yet to pull up his trousers, piped up.

"Only ladies?" he pouted.

"Whatever, you heart desires," said Beauderriere.

"Count me in," said the floral shirt bedecked sailor.

"Count us all in, Hurrah!" they all shouted. Beauderriere beamed.

"Meet me on the docks at dawn, hurrah!" he bawled. "Hurrah," they all replied.

Beauderriere left the inn and made his way to the Royal Palace. As he approached the palace, he saw Columbus walking towards him.

"I have the ships," shouted Columbus.

"Oh, what a shame, it must be all that fruit you eat!" said Beauderriere.

"Not shits, ships, I have the ships!"

"And I have a load of sailors!" replied Beauderriere, getting some strange looks from passers-by.

"We must go and look at the ships!" shouted Columbus.

Beauderriere followed Columbus back to the docks and soon they gazed upon the three ships that would take them across the Atlantic Ocean. There they were, given by gracious donation by King Ferdinand and Queen Isabella.

"What a load of nautical rubbish!" said Beauderriere.

"We were lucky to get them, they were going off on a voyage," said Columbus.

"Where were they off to, the knackers yard?" sneered Beauderriere. Columbus stared at the ships.

"They need a little work granted, nothing that a little sail and nail wouldn't cure."

"I was thinking of something like…a fire, what are they called?" said Beauderriere.

"They are the Colander, the Drain and the Gully, fine names for three soon-to-be fine ships."

"Well, I jolly well hope so," bemoaned Beauderriere. Columbus turned to Beauderriere.

"Well, I've got the ships, where is the crew?" he asked.

"Fifty of the finest sailors alive will be here at dawn tomorrow!" said Beauderriere.

"Where did you find them at such short notice?" asked Columbus.

"I found them in an inn," said Beauderriere proudly.

"I hope you didn't get any of those mutinous bastards from the 'Galloping Pox' inn."

"No…no, they are all fine upstanding sea dogs," said Beauderriere cautiously.

"Good, good," said Columbus.

"Why wouldn't you want any sailors from the 'Galloping Pox' inn?" asked Beauderriere. Columbus stared out at sea.

"A friend of mine," began Columbus, "Captain Velasquez, sailed his ship, manned by men from the 'Galloping Pox' inn into the Mediterranean, with him he had his wife, his mother-in-law and his mother-in-law's little dog. They hadn't gone far when the crew mutinied, raped the women, and the dog, and some vicious swine in a floral shirt raped the Captain, then they strung them up on the yardarm, dog and all."

"I...see...,"said Beauderriere.

"If I ever see them again, I'll kill them myself!" promised Columbus.

"I...see," said Beauderriere, "look, I'll sort out the ships, and you concentrate on the maps and buy the provisions and all that stuff."

"Good idea," said Columbus, "I'll see you in three weeks; we should be ready to sail by then."

With the ships repaired, provisioned and manned, the intrepid travellers set sail. After several weeks of sailing, the crew were beginning to turn ugly, especially the one in the floral shirt. Beauderriere went to Columbus' cabin.

"I think the crew are revolting," said Beauderriere.

"Of course they are," said Columbus, "filthy lot, especially that one in the floral shirt."

"No, I mean, they are getting edgy, we've been sailing for a long time and no sight of land."

Columbus stood up and went to his charts.

"We are on course, shouldn't be long now," he said. Beauderriere looked at the charts and an overwhelming feeling came over him.

"I have an idea that we should make a forty-five degree turns about now," he said.

"What makes you suggest that!" asked Columbus.

"Well, I come from a long line of navigators," said Beauderriere, "and I believe I'm right."
Columbus thought for a moment and banged the chart table.

"I trust you implicitly Beauderriere, we'll make that left turn."

So that is what they did, and the world was to hear no more of the intrepid adventures of Derek Columbus, we would have to wait until his nephew Christopher tried his hand.

AUTHORS NOTES ON THIS CHAPTER
Nope..nothing!

Chapter Eleven
I Did What With My What!

Now, King Henry the Eighth had been married to Queen Catherine of Aragon for over twenty years. He was rather perturbed that he had not yet got a son and heir.

He resolved that problem by divorcing her and breaking away from the Church in Rome. He married Anne Boleyn, and she gave birth to a daughter, the future Queen Elizabeth I. Once again, he was without a son and heir. He sat in conference with his advisors.

"I do not know how we can help Your Majesty!" said the Duke of Norfolk.

"Something must be done, I must have a son to reign after me!" shouted the King. The advisors looked at each other.

"Perhaps, her Majesty will give you the son you desire," said the Archbishop.

"I think not, Archbishop, not now, she is fast becoming unbearable to me!" said the King.

"But, you have the Princess Mary and Princess Elizabeth, to follow after you, Sire," pleaded the Archbishop, "more pious and faithful daughters than anyone could have." The King stood up and paced the room.

"They are not sons!"

"Well, I don't know, Mary has a little moustache… I don't know what can be done, Sire," said Norfolk.

"I do, I will divorce the Queen, and marry someone who can give me a son!" he stormed. The Archbishop padded over to the King.

"You cannot do that, Sire."

The King turned on the Archbishop and took him by the scruff of his neck.

"You dare to tell me… Me! What I can and cannot do!" he screamed.

"No... No, of course not, Sire!" pleaded the Archbishop, "I would never do that, but I don't think the people will tolerate another divorce!" The King let go of the Archbishop

"Then what can I do?" he said. The Duke of Norfolk stood up and walked over to the King.

"It's a shame, your Majesty, that the Queen is so very faithful to you, isn't it?" he said.

The King and Norfolk looked at each other for a moment, then the King dismissed the others and he and Norfolk sat down.

"What are you saying, Thomas?" inquired the King.

"Wouldn't it all be very simple if the Queen had...shall we say... an involvement, Sire?"

"Go on, Thomas."

"If Her Majesty were...involved with someone, you would have every right to...dispose of her, Sire."

"But, the Queen would not do that, would she?"

"Of course not," Your Majesty, but with a little encouragement...!"

"Tell me more," said the King. Norfolk put his finger to his lips.

"I think it best, that you are unaware of any plans, your Majesty, if you know nothing, you can remain impartial," said Norfolk.

"So be it, Thomas," said the King, "I'll leave it all up to you." Norfolk bowed and walked to the door. The King called out after him.

"If this fails, Thomas, I will have your head!" Norfolk bowed again and left the room.

Lord Beauderriere was out hunting on his estate when the news came to him that the Duke of Norfolk was at Tanners Hall and was waiting upon him.

The hunting party rode back and soon Beauderriere was seated, drinking wine with the Duke.

"You have a fine house, Beauderriere," said Norfolk, and a very fine cellar." Norfolk drained his glass, which was soon refilled.

"You are very kind, sir," said Beauderriere, "may I ask the purpose of your visit?"

Norfolk took another sip from his glass and looked at Beauderriere. "You have been noticed at Court, by some very high-ranking people," said Norfolk.

"That's very nice, might I ask who?" inquired Beauderriere.

"None other than the Queen herself!" said Norfolk with a wink.

"I see, I am very honoured," said Beauderriere.

"She has asked me to tell you that she wishes that your become her 'Gentleman of the Bedchamber'"

"A great honour, indeed," said Beauderriere.

The Duke of Norfolk stood up and walked towards the door. "She expects you within the week," he said. The two gentlemen bowed and Norfolk left.

One week later, Beauderriere was at Hampton Court. He was shown into the Queen's Presence Chamber.

"My Lord Beauderriere," she said, "you are to be my new Gentleman of the Bedchamber."

"A great honour, your Majesty," said Beauderriere, bowing low.

"I suppose you realise, my lord, that this post means you spending quite a lot of time with me alone in my bedchamber," said the Queen.

"Yes, Your Majesty, I realise that."

"You will become very intimate with many of my private parts," said the Queen.

"I can assure Your Majesty, that I will make sure that my hands are warm at all times," said Beauderriere.

The weeks passed and one morning the Queen and Beauderriere were admiring some needlework the Queen had just finished.

Outside of the door stood Mistress Golightly, she had her ear to the door. What she heard was given in evidence at Beauderriere's trial.

Beauderriere was taken to the Tower and then brought before the Duke of Norfolk and the Court. Mistress Golightly was brought in to give evidence.

"Now, Mistress Golightly, tell me word for word, all that you overheard," said Norfolk.

"Well sir, the first thing I heard was the rustling of material, and the Queen said 'What do you think of that, my lord' and Lord Beauderriere replied, 'It looks lovely, let me have a closer look,' there was a lot of giggling and then there was some more material rustling and Lord Beauderriere said 'What do you think of that' and the Queen said laughing, 'It's massive, I think I will need both hands to hold it'" informed Mistress Golightly.

"I see," said Norfolk. Beauderriere stood and spoke to the Court.

"We were just comparing our needlework, that's all," he countered. Norfolk waved away Beauderriere's remonstrations and turned to Mistress Golightly.

"Carry on," said Norfolk.

"Well, sir, then I heard Lord Beauderriere say, 'Perhaps if I put it here, you won't have to hold it for long.' There were a few moments of silence then I heard the Queen, who seemed out of breath, say, 'Mmm, that fits just right'" Beauderriere stood up again.

"This is a farce, my needlework was large and heavy, I placed in the Queen's rack so she could admire it better," he said. Norfolk turned on Beauderriere.

"I have sworn statements from diverse persons that you did plunder her inner warmth with your massive prod."

"I don't understand," said Beauderriere, "I did what with my what?"

The Duke of Norfolk was walking in the courtyard with the King.

"Well," said the King, "how did it go?"

"The man is obviously some kind of pervert," replied Norfolk, "he referred to his member as 'needlework' and Her Majesty's private parts as a 'rack'"

"I see, so he admitted adultery with the Queen," the King said sorrowfully.

"Eventually," said Norfolk, "he needed some encouragement from Your Majesty's torturers."

"They must both go to the block," said the King, "I must find another wife, someone who will be true, and faithful."

"Yes, we must start looking for number three, straight away!"

"And then I shall be at peace," said the King, "and will spend the rest of my life with her!"

AUTHORS NOTES ON THIS CHAPTER
I am quite sure that Beauderriere almost admitted it when the word 'massive' was mentioned!

Chapter Twelve
Virgin On The Ridiculous

She was more of a man than her father. She could make you shit a brick just by looking at you. Queen Elizabeth I was sitting astride her horse at Tilbury just before the navy left port to fight the Spanish Armada.

"I may have the body of a weak and feeble woman!" she shouted.

A voice came from the back of the crowd. "Nice tits though!"

"Thank you," replied the Queen, "but I have the heart of a King, and a King of England too!"

"Nice arse as well!" came the voice. "You're too kind!" smiled Elizabeth.

Elizabeth had gone through such a lot in her life. She was now Queen of England, and she used her position to make her mark in the world. She was receiving marriage proposals from every realm in Christendom.

She dallied with a few admirers, but her heart was set on one man, James, Lord Beauderriere, son of her mother's supposed lover.

Her other admirers included, Sir Francis Drake, Sir Walter Raleigh, the Earl of Leicester and the Earl of Essex. Sir Francis Drake was one of the nation's heroes; he had circumnavigated the world, singed the King of Spain's beard, and brought Spanish gold to fill England's dwindling coffers.

Sir Walter Raleigh had brought potatoes, tobacco, and some gold. The Earl of Leicester had just given himself to the Queen's service and the Earl of Essex had brought nothing but trouble.

Elizabeth would flirt and talk with them all. However, she reserved her total admiration for Beauderriere who would often visit the Queen in her quarters.

"I hope Your Majesty had a pleasant day," asked Beauderriere.

"Oh, the usual, meetings with my advisors, ambassadors," she said, "it's nice to relax with a good friend, James." She smiled at Beauderriere and moved closer.

"I suppose you are familiar with your family tradition," said the Queen.

"My family tradition?" said Beauderriere.

"Your father and my mother, James," said the Queen, seductively, "their needle working."

Beauderriere shifted uncomfortably from one foot to the other.

"I did hear of such a thing," said Beauderriere, "but surely it was all lies, so that your father could marry Queen Jane Seymour."

"Lies or not," said the Queen, "we all like a bit of 'needle working' after a long day."

Soon the Queen and Beauderriere were at it like knives, and later, they sat back and Beauderriere lit up a pipe.

"I must say," he said between puffs, "this is perhaps the one good thing that Raleigh has ever brought back."

"Yes," said the Queen, munching on a potato, "Much better than these things, give us a drag!"

"It seems that Sir Francis Drake wants to circumnavigate the globe again," began the Queen, "and this time he wants you to captain one of his ships."

Beauderriere coughed violently as the smoke from his pipe choked him. "Me!" spluttered Beauderriere, "Why me?" The Queen stood up and walked to the window.

"It seems," she said, "that Sir Francis has heard that you family were renowned sailors and navigators." Beauderriere spluttered again.

"Sailors and navigators, they were the biggest bunch of tossers around!"

"Nevertheless," continued the Queen, "I have given him permission to take you with him."

Beauderriere knew that the Queen would not change her mind, he also knew that she had been eyeing up Raleigh's well-filled tights.

One cold and wet morning, Beauderriere met Drake on the docks.

"Good morrow!" called out Drake, "welcome to the expedition!"

"Whatever," said Beauderriere.

"We will leave on the early morning tide," said Drake taking a deep breath. "We will be three ships, I will have that one, 'The Sturdy Vessel', Captain Hawkins will have that one, 'The Solid Sailor', and you will have that one, 'The Leaky Sieve'"

"Wonderful, just bleeding wonderful," said Beauderriere.

Drake clapped Beauderriere on the back. "I've also rounded you a fine crew, got them from 'The Galloping Pox' inn," said Drake, "They look a good crew."

Beauderriere had a little touch of deja vu but shook it off.

Upon their return from their trip, Drake and Hawkins had to inform the Queen of the sad loss of Beauderriere.

"Tell me what happened," asked the Queen.

"Well, Your Majesty," began Drake, "we were approaching Cape Horn, when without any reason whatsoever, Beauderriere ordered his ship to make a 45° turn to the left, and..."

AUTHORS NOTES ON THIS CHAPTER

Some of this chapter is quite plausible. Did you see the link with the previous chapter, it just shows how much I am concentrating as I write this book.

Chapter Thirteen
Alas Poor William

Not many of the Beauderriere family had any literary bent, the majority of them could not read or write, but one of them achieved fame as the greatest playwright of them all, yes, you've guessed it, William Beauderriere Shakespeare.

William left his father's house and travelled to London. As he wandered through the grimy Elizabethan streets, he was attracted by the sounds coming from a great circular building in Southwark.

He purchased a ticket and became enthralled as he discovered that the place was a theatre. After an enjoyable evening watching plays he decided that this life was for him.

His first play was called *'Whoops Mrs Windsor, Why So Merry'* a farce. This did not do very well, nor his other plays he produced; *'Come, Lady Essex, Show Us Your Arse'* and *'Much Ado About Bugger All'*.

As he sat one day in an alehouse, a man walked up to him and sat down.

"You seem rather sad Sir, are you adverse to company?"

"No," said William, "I'm just a little disappointed at my performances." The man raised his eyebrow and moved closer to William.

"May I introduce myself; I am Christopher Marlowe, playwright, actor and well-known shirt lifter. May I have the pleasure to know to whom I am talking?"

"I am sir, William Beauderriere Shakespeare, playwright, actor and one who likes to sit on his shirt tails.

"I think sir," said Marlowe, "that we must collaborate."

"What do you have in mind?" asked William. Marlowe and William were walking by the Thames.

"It is my belief, began Marlowe, "that no one man can be responsible for great works, they must be the product of a collective mind, which is why I think that you and I should put our heads together." William looked at him warily.

"Let me get this straight, when you say we should put our heads together, you mean, our writing heads, not the heads of our penises."

Marlowe laughed a strange high-pitched laugh.

"Willy," he began, "Willy, Willy, Willy, I mean business."

"Yes, I've heard about how you go about your 'business', I want none of it."

Marlowe walked over to the riverbank and sat down. William waited a while and then sat down next to him.

"Look Will," began Marlowe, "I have a confession to make; I'm not what you think I am." William looked relieved and sat nearer to Marlowe.

"You mean you're not one for the men, thank goodness for that." Marlowe put his arm around Will's shoulder.

"That's not what I meant," said Marlowe, and will try anything to get my hand on your codpiece, what I was going to say is that I am not just a playwright, I am also a spy!"

William extricated himself from Marlowe's embrace and stood up.

"A spy, a spy for whom, not the Spaniards." William began to panic, "Oh my God I'll be hung drawn and quartered."

"I am not a spy for the Spaniards; I work for the English, Lord Walsingham to be exact." Marlowe stood up

"I need you to help me, I need you to act as my literary agent, and get my plays produced as I am going abroad for quite a while."

"I can do that," began William, "but won't it look funny if you name is put to them, it will keep you at a high profile, you will be sought out to take the accolades."

"Yes, good thinking Will, I never thought of that…I know, put your name to them, as long as I get the money, or a fair portion of it, I am quite happy and I will be able to carry on my work for the government, you're a true friend Will."

Marlowe handed Will an enormous portfolio of his work and then disappeared into the night telling Will that he will be in touch.

Marlowe never did get in touch, he was murdered the next week, so William decided that he won't mention to anyone that the work he was producing was not his, but Christopher Marlowe's.

Soon the London stage was ringing with applause for this wonderful new playwright, William Shakespeare.

AUTHORS NOTES ON THIS CHAPTER

There is a large faction of academics who believe that William Shakespeare was not the author of the plays attributed to him. This may be the answer.....or not!

Chapter Fourteen
Divided By Gunpowder Treason & Porn

By the time of the English Civil War, the then scion of the House of Beauderriere had been elevated to an earldom. Sir Flagellant Beauderriere had become the first Earl of Beauderriere. A staunch Royalist at the start of the Civil War, he supported and fought for his King. One day he was summoned into the King's presence.

"Ah, Beauderriere, I have a task for you," said the King.

"Your wish is my command Sire."

The King put his arm around his shoulders and they walked away from the others.

"My dear Beauderriere, I need you to make a heroic gesture. Things are looking pretty bad for me and I need one of my ablest commanders to take the fight to Cromwell," the King said quietly. Lord Beauderriere's chest swelled.

"Unfortunately," continued the king, "all of my most able commanders are dead or have defected; you are the only commander left."

"What did you have in mind, Sire?" asked Beauderriere.

"I will leave the details to you, gather around you those you can trust and ride to London and take Parliament," the King said.

"And that's all," said Beauderriere rather sarcastically.
Beauderriere gathered around him some of the times most ablest men and their commanders he could find, General Vauxhall's Cavaliers, Colonel Ford's Escorts and Lord Morris' D'Ancers.

He called his commanders to his quarters. He looked at his men; Lord Morris, a cousin, was bereft of style and élan. General Vauxhall, a bluff Yorkshireman and Colonel Ford, a strange looking individual, with an uncommon taste dressing in women's clothing, sometimes when it was not even needed.

"We have monumental task gentlemen, but I think we are up to it," began Beauderriere.

"We can do anything, my lord, anything, except of course, going to London and taking over Parliament," said General Vauxhall.

"Yes," interjected Lord Morris. "That's the only thing we cannot do." Colonel Ford agreed, adjusting his bonnet.

"Oh, no, we can't do that, I have nothing to wear for that."

"Well, Beauderriere," said Lord Morris, "what does His Majesty want us to do?" Lord Beauderriere sat staring at his men.

"I have been asked by the King, to undertake a special task, I have chosen the best men for it."

"Well, bring them in so we can go home," said Lord Morris.

"Yes, don't waste your time with us three losers," said General Vauxhall, "Not if you've got something to do."

"Will you just listen!" shouted Beauderriere.

"We're good at listening," said Colonel Ford, I got a first for listening at school, oh, and Prep, I think you'll find that I can speak it like a native." Lord Beauderriere banged his fist on the table.

"Shut up, shut up!" he shouted.

"Ooooh, get him!" said Lord Morris. A look from Beauderriere soon silenced them.

"Our task is to go to London and take Parliament, what say you?" The three men nodded and agreed that they could easily do that, "but, you just told me...Oh, bollocks!"

The three men said they would follow Lord Beauderriere to the ends of the earth. Most of them stayed with him until he reached the end of his drive, but they were soon of looking for plunder.

Mrs Plunder ran a brothel and always welcomed soldiers. Lord Beauderriere spent the rest of the war changing sides as often as he changed his underwear - twice.

During this period, there was a lot of unrest in England, religion fought religion and it culminated with was has become to be known as the Gunpowder Plot.

History tells us that Guy Fawkes, or to give him his actual name, Guy Beauderriere-Fawkes, attempted to blow up King and Parliament. Fawkes was the son of the youngest daughter of the then Earl of Beauderriere.

He was discovered under the Houses of Parliament with barrels of gunpowder. The Beauderriere Documents now tell us that the only thing explosive in those barrels was twofold.

Fawkes had discovered something he called 'flash powder' which could be used in taking photographs in subdued light, but as photography had not yet been invented, there was no real use for it yet.

He rented the vaults under Parliament to store the barrels until he could find a use for it. He stored it next to some boxes that were already there.

When he was found, he was arrested and we all know what happened to him, but he was not hanged, drawn, and quartered for treason, but to keep his mouth shut. We now come to the second explosive part.

In those boxes were the hottest pornographic magazines and sketches secreted there by the Members of Parliaments for those long nights of debate. Even today, just before the opening of Parliament the vaults are checked, they do not want to have their stash found, especially them, as the November issue is always red-hot.

AUTHORS NOTES ON THIS CHAPTER
Yeah..right....crap wasn't it?

Chapter Fifteen
A Fishy Tale

As I mentioned previously, Lord Beauderriere changed sides in the Civil War twice, this was one of the times. Although I must just mention that this was not one of the times he changed his underwear.

Beauderriere managed this change at a rather fortuitous moment. He was hiding in the house of Lord Gullible, a friend of his, when the door burst open and a troop of Roundheads came in. Quick as a flash, he took out his pistol and hit his friend over the head.

"Take that you Royalist dog!" he said. He turned to the Captain of the Roundheads.

"There, Captain, another Royalist for the Tower!"

The Captain slapped Beauderriere on the back.

"Well done, comrade, we've been after this one for a long time, General Cromwell will be pleased with your work."

"Oliver Cromwell!" gasped Beauderriere, "yes, let us take this wretch to him now."

The Roundheads and Beauderriere, with Lord Gullible across his horse, entered London. During the journey, Lord Gullible had come to every now and then, only to be sent back to an unconscious state by a rap of Beauderriere's pistol butt.

Soon they were in the august presence of Oliver Cromwell. He was standing at a table covered with maps, the table, not Cromwell, surrounded by his Generals. Cromwell looked up as the Captain and Beauderriere entered the room.

"What is your report, Captain," said Cromwell, "have you caught Gullible yet?"

"Yes, Sir," informed the Captain, "with the help of this loyal Parliamentarian, Lord Beauderriere." Cromwell looked at Beauderriere.

"You have my thanks; Gullible is the last of the traitors. Beauderriere slowly crept up to Cromwell.

"Look, he may start going on about me not being a Parliamentarian and that I am really his friend and a loyal subject of the King, well he's bound to say that, isn't he?"

"Have no fear, he will say nothing, he'll go straight to the block and that's that!"

"Oh, shit, poor old Gullible, oh well, never mind." Cromwell ordered the others out of the room, he and Beauderriere went over to the table, and Cromwell poured them each a glass of wine.

"We have bigger fish than Gullible to fry, my lord," said Cromwell, "much bigger fish."

"Well, I am rather peckish…" Cromwell looked strangely at Beauderriere and then laughed.

"You are a cool customer, my lord, I like that!"

"Sorry," asked Beauderriere.

"We are all peckish for the big fish, my lord, and we have him!"

"Him, General?" queried Beauderriere.

"We have our biggest fish." Beauderriere stared at Cromwell in amazement.

"But, the question is," mused Cromwell, "what to do with him, now we have him."

The thought of a large fish, dripping in butter filled Beauderriere's head. He hadn't the chance to eat at Lord Gullible's before the soldiers came. Cromwell's voice brought him out of his reverie.

"What should we do first?" he asked.

"Well, the only thing to do is to cut off his head, gut him, smear him with butter and roast him over a slow fire," Beauderriere said licking his lips. Cromwell looked at Beauderriere aghast.

"You're a strange one, my lord, but I see what you mean."

Cromwell went around the table and after a little thought, signed a large sheet of paper; Beauderriere thought he had seen the words 'Death Warrant' at the top. Cromwell turned back to Beauderriere.

"You may return to your estates, we may have need for you later," said Cromwell.

Beauderriere left the room and Cromwell's officers returned. Cromwell looked at them.

"You remember we were going to send the King to exile in France?" said Cromwell." The others nodded in agreement.

"Well, after a discussion with a far greater man than I, I have decided that the King must face the executioner."

The others began to remonstrate with Cromwell; I think we will leave them at it.

AUTHORS NOTES ON THIS CHAPTER
I like this chapter. These authors notes don't have to be long! It is what the author thinks about the chapter!!

Chapter Sixteen
A Plague And A Fire

The Beauderrieres return to the annals of history was during the Reformation, when King Charles II sat on the throne. After a bloodbath, nothing was left of the Roundheads who had killed his father, apart from Lord Beauderriere that is. We find Lord Beauderriere kneeling in front of the King.

"Your Majesty, I fought and fought, but Lord Gullible knocked me unconscious and I was taken, I only just escaped with my life."

The King got up from his throne and raised Beauderriere to his feet.

"My brave, loyal Beauderriere, how can I repay you?"

"To see you sitting on your father's throne is payment enough, Your Majesty."

"I do not think so," said the King, "I hereby decree that the lands and property of that traitor, Lord Gullible, be handed over to my loyal friend, Lord Beauderriere, and I think it is scant reward!"

Beauderriere returned to his estates and basked in the glory of his King's regard.

There was a pestilence beginning to cover the land, people were dying, and no one knew why. Soon everyone would know the plague. The whole country was soon in the grip of this terrible sickness.

Our hero was trapped in Tanners Hall, not wanting to leave. Beauderriere who spent the daylight hours sitting in his highest turret shot anybody who approached the Hall. He had his men place mantraps all around the Hall, and when his men returned from laying them, he shot them.

He actually shot everyone who came into musket range, including, his father-in-law, his mother-in-law, a passing tinker, and the man who had come to tell him that the plague was over.

The message was finally sent after Beauderriere had run out of ammunition. The man that delivered the message was, on Beauderriere's orders, stabbed to death, just in case.

Beauderriere decided it was time to return to court, so he loaded up his furniture and headed off to London. He arrived at his town house and settled in. His wife, as usual was left behind at Tanners Hall, he didn't want her to cramp his style while he was in the big city. As soon as he was ready, he decided to go out for a walk.

He made his way through the streets of London and soon found himself in an area of London with which he was not familiar.

He was soon accosted by various locals offering him a variety of things, from oysters to a quick shag. As he wandered down a dark dimly lit street, he came to a bakers shop. He entered the shop.

"I say, baker chappie, I'm feeling peckish, what have you for me to eat?"

"I'm closing now sir, I've just dampened down my oven and I've nothing until the morning."

"Come on, my good man, said Beauderriere, "you must be able to prepare me something, a pie or some such." The baker looked around his shop.

"I suppose I can put a few glowing ashes in this rather wonky brazier and put this pie on it."

"That would be admirable, my man," said Beauderriere.

"I'll have to put it outside the shop as I must close now."

Beauderriere stood next to the brazier waiting for his pie to heat up. Soon it was ready and he gently picked it up with his cloak and moved off.

As he went away, the edge of his cloak caught on the brazier and pulled it over and it fell down into the baker's cellar. Beauderriere ignored this and walked on eating his pie.

In the early hours of the morning, Beauderriere was woken up by shouting and screaming. He got up and went to his window, opened it and called to a man passing below.

"You there, what's all this noise?"

The man doffed his cap. "If it pleases your Lordship, London is ablaze!"

"Ablaze, what do you mean?"

"It's all on fire, started in a bakers cellar in Pudding Lane!"

Beauderriere cast his mind back to his pie, and blushed; his blush was hidden from the man by the glow of the fire. "Is it coming this way?" asked Beauderriere.

"No, the river will stop it, said the man. " The King is out on the streets, he is directing the fire fighters." Beauderriere closed the window and hurriedly dressed. He left his house and headed for the fire.

As he reached the conflagration, he saw the King talking to man. Beauderriere walked up to the King and bowed low.

"Your Majesty, what a terrible disaster to befall us," said Beauderriere.

The King bowed back. "Yes, my lord, and so soon after the plague," replied the King.

"Yes, but perhaps this inferno will wipe out all remnants of that pestilence," said Beauderriere.

"A very good point, my lord, perhaps we should congratulate whoever started it," said the King. Beauderriere thought for a moment.

"Well, I..." began Beauderriere.

"And when I have thanked him," continued the King, "I will cut off his head for causing such destruction... I'm sorry, my lord, you were going to say?"

"Nothing, nothing whatsoever, Your Majesty."

AUTHORS NOTES ON THIS CHAPTER
And this one, they're sort of linked aren't they, very clever.

Chapter Seventeen
Bonnie Wee Laddie

Lord Beauderriere had decided to go and visit his estates in Scotland. He had heard about the Jacobite Rebellion, but he was only interested in collecting his rents.

He stopped his horse outside one of his tenants' hovels; he dismounted and opened the door.

"McDonald!" he shouted, "I've come for my money"

As he looked around the dank, dark room, he saw a woman asleep in the corner on a mattress of straw.

"I say, my good woman," he boomed, "Where's that rascal, McDonald."

The woman woke and swung her legs off the bed and Beauderriere noticed that she was wearing men's riding boots. She looked flustered.

"Och, I think he's away with his sheep," she replied. Beauderriere had a picture of McDonald up on the hills shagging his sheep, but a shake of the head cleared it.

"I'm Lord Beauderriere, I need to see him, and I'll wait." Beauderriere sat down at a table and looked at the strange woman. She may look a bit masculine, but something attracted him to her.

"So, are you related to McDonald, young lady?"

"Och, no, sir, I am friend of his daughter, Lurpak," she replied.

"You mean Flora."

"Aye, Flora, that's it."

"What's your name, my pretty?" ask Beauderriere.

"Charlie," came the reply.

"Charlie, that's a boy's name," queried Beauderriere.

"It's...it's short for Charlotte," she said.

At that moment, the door opened and five Scotsmen entered, resplendent in their tartan. Charlotte stood up and the five men shouted in unison.

"Hurrah, for Bonnie Prince Charlie!" Beauderriere stood and drew his sword.

"Who, where, what did you say?" he blustered.

The men all looked at the girl (who you must have now realised is Bonnie Prince Charlie in drag.) Then they looked at Beauderriere standing there, with his sword drawn.

"We said... began the first man.

"Yes," said Beauderriere.

"That we liked her dress and that...," said the second man.

"Yes," said Beauderriere.

"We liked the prints on the dress, they are bonny," said the third man.

"Yes," said Beauderriere.

"And her name's..." said the fourth man.

"Charlie, yes," said Beauderriere.

"So, we all remarked...,"said the fifth man.

"Bonnie... Prints... Charlie!" said all five together.

Beauderriere sheathed his sword and sat down. "Well, that's cleared that up," said Beauderriere, "I thought you had said, Bonnie Prince Charlie."

The five men laughed nervously. "That would be silly, wouldn't it?" said the first man.

"It would indeed," said Beauderriere, taking a pistol from his belt, "if he was here, I'd blow his pissing head off!"

The five men and Charlie all laughed nervously. "Well, Charlie," said the second man, "the boats ready and Flora's waiting for you."

Beauderriere stood up. "So, you're off then?" he said.

"Yes, I'm going over the sea to Skye," said Charlie, "with Mr McDonald's daughter, Margarine."

"Flora, you mean."

"Yes, yes, damn it, Flora."

"Oh, well, Bon Voyage."

The five men and Charlie stumbled over each other to get out of the room. A little while later, Mr. McDonald came into the room, and was taken aback to see Beauderriere. He looked around the room.

"She's gone," said Beauderriere, "over the sea to Skye with your daughter, Clover."

"You mean Flora," said McDonald.

"Flora, yes, strange girl, that Charlie, she seemed to have a little bit more than other girls."

"Aye!"

AUTHORS NOTES ON THIS CHAPTER
For those readers who do not quite get the joke about the name changes of Flora, they are all butter-related spreads as is Flora.

Chapter Eighteen
Go On Horatio, Where Your Medals

It was understood, that as an ancestor of his had sailed to America with Columbus, Tarquin Beauderriere would have salt in his blood. He didn't, when he was assigned to H.M.S. Victory in 1805, he wasn't sure if he had any blood in his veins, he didn't have anything in his stomach that's for sure.

As the ship crossed the Bay of Biscay en route to Trafalgar, Beauderriere spent most of his time in his cabin or leaning over the side.

His face had assumed such a strange pallor that that certain shade of green went down in history as 'Beauderriere Green'.

As he pushed himself away from the ships rail for the umpteenth time, he heard someone in the crow's nest called out.

"Ship, Ahoy! It's the French."
Soon everyone was rushing about trying to get to their battle stations. Beauderriere made his way below deck and went to the Admiral's cabin. He knocked and entered.

"The French have been sighted, Admiral!" said Beauderriere.

Nelson was on his bed with Captain Hardy. They sat up quickly.

"Good, good," said Nelson, "we will soon engage them."

"Where do you think would be the best place to meet them, Horatio?" asked Beauderriere.
Nelson looked at his charts.

"This looks a good spot, Cape Trafalgar, this I think will be my greatest victory!" he said.

"I wonder what part of your anatomy you will lose this time, Horatio?" asked Beauderriere.

"Not much left, old boy," said Nelson whimsically. Nelson walked Beauderriere to a corner.

"Do you think we should make a forty-five degree turn to the left Tarquin?" asked Nelson, Beauderriere shook his head.

"I can see no earthly reason why we should do that Horatio." replied Beauderriere.

"You are absolutely sure."

"Absolutely!" said Beauderriere.

"Right, let's get at those French!" Nelson exclaimed. Captain Hardy moved over to Nelson.

"I think it would be best if you stayed below decks Horatio, it could be dangerous!" said Hardy anxiously.

"Bollocks," said Beauderriere.

"I think it would be safer, if the Admiral were to remain here!" said Hardy angrily.

"Oh, and you could stay here with him, couldn't you?" sneered Beauderriere.

"If he wanted me to!" said Hardy, looking expectantly at Nelson.

"Ignore him Horatio, go on, get up there, and wear all your medals, show these buggers who you are!" encouraged Beauderriere. Very soon, the three men were up on deck.

"I think you should hide behind these barrels, Horatio," suggested Hardy.

"Bollocks," shouted Beauderriere, "stand right out in the middle, let the men see you're right with them."

Hardy tried to make Nelson hide away, but Nelson listened to Beauderriere.

Soon the battle was raging, cannon balls were flying everywhere, and up in the rigging of one of the French ships, a man with a musket was surveying the deck of H.M.S. Victory.

He saw Nelson standing there, resplendent in his Admirals' uniform and with his medals glinting. The man fired his musket and Nelson fell. Beauderriere and Hardy knelt beside him

"Take me below decks," said Nelson, "I don't want the men to see that I have fallen, I don't want them to be discouraged."

Beauderriere covered Nelson with his cloak and lifted him up and walked to the hatch.

"Out of the way you men, dying Admiral coming through!" Beauderriere shouted. They laid Nelson on some sacking and made him comfortable.

"Where does it hurt, Horatio?" asked Beauderriere.

"Everywhere," said Nelson, "but especially on my head when you smacked it against the bleeding hatch when you were bringing me down here!" Hardy soon joined them.

"Admiral, the battle is going our way, you have a great victory," he said.

"Thank the Lord for that," said Beauderriere. Nelson turned to Hardy.

"Kiss me, Hardy," he said. Hardy took Nelson's head in his hands and gave him a big wet kiss on the lips. Nelson passed away.

"What did you do that for!" said Beauderriere.

"He asked me to kiss him," said Hardy.

"I think you'll find that he said 'Kismet, Hardy!' said Beauderriere, "not feel my tonsils with your tongue!"

"I know what I heard!" said Hardy smiling.

"Yes, I know, what do we do with him now?" said Beauderriere.

"Stick him in a barrel of Brandy to preserve him," said Hardy with a look in his eye, "and then perhaps we could go down to my cabin for some 'Kismet' "I don't mind if I do!" said Beauderriere with a wink.

<u>AUTHORS NOTES ON THIS CHAPTER</u>
Another great chapter....god! I'm good aren't I?

Chapter Nineteen
Beauderriere Meets His Waterloo

All Europe was under the heel of Napoleon. He had been captured once and imprisoned on the island of Elba. Now he was free again. Opposite him stood the formidable army of The Duke of Wellington. The Duke called all of his commanding officers into his tent for a pre-battle briefing.

"Tomorrow will be the day that decides the future of Europe," said Wellington, "we must be ready."

His generals chorused that they were all ready, except General Beauderriere.

"What's your problem, Beauderriere?" demanded Wellington.

"Well, I don't know if you remember," said Beauderriere, "but you said I could have a couple of weeks off in June, so I won't be here."

"Won't be here, what the hell are you talking about!" screamed Wellington. Beauderriere moved meekly through the other officers.

"I always have a couple of weeks off in June, you know, for the Beauderriere Virgins Fair," said Beauderriere timidly.

"Don't be so bleeding ridiculous, we will need your heavy cannon during the battle!"

"I like to think that my 'heavy cannon' will be rather busy at the fair," said Beauderriere using a lot of double entende.

Wellington dismissed the other officers and advanced on Beauderriere.

"Ever since you joined my brigade, you have been nothing but a pain in the neck," began Wellington, "you do nothing but whine about the sleeping quarters, about the bugler in the mornings, about having to transport your cannon in training, about everything, and I'm getting sick of it!"

"Well, it's nothing like it said it would be in the brochures," said Beauderriere, "no swimming, skiing, or partially clad young ladies."

"How would we recruit anyone if the brochures told the truth, join the army and get your bloody head blown off!" said Wellington.

The two men stood looking at one another for a while.

"So, what about the Virgins Fair," said Beauderriere, "if I leave now, I will just make it."

Wellington fumed for a moment. "If I let you go, you will have to leave your cannon behind!"

"Well, I was going to put a show on at the Virgins Fair, sort of military tattoo, y'know, but, if you think you'll need them, I leave them."

"How very kind of you," said Wellington, "well I hope you have a lovely time, hope the weather holds!" Beauderriere starts to leave.

"Oh," said Beauderriere, I've invited my friend Marshal Blucher to come over and see you; he may be of help to you."

"Thank you, oh, and Beauderriere, if I ever see your stupid bloody face ever again, I smash the bleeding thing in!"

Beauderriere mounted his horse and started to ride off. His batman ran up to him.

"Where are you off to, my lord?"

"I've got to pop home for a bit of business, but I'll be stopping of at Waterloo for a few days, nice young lady there, I expect there will be fireworks!" Beauderriere spurred on his horse.

AUTHORS NOTES ON THIS CHAPTER
Did you see the reference to the Virgins Fair?

Chapter Twenty
Into The Valley of Death

Lord Beauderriere was always slightly peeved that his name did not go down in history as the others great generals of the Crimea. Lord Raglan had his sleeve; Lord Cardigan had his nice warm woolly...um...Cardigan I suppose. Even the place gave its name to a head covering.

Beauderriere thought that something must be named after him, because at several times he had seen one of his soldiers pick up a shovel and some paper and say 'I'm going for a Beauderriere'.

Well, enough of this badinage and wit, we must concentrate on the battle. Lord Cardigan had called his generals together to discuss the growing problems.

"My lord," said Lord Raglan, adjusting his sleeve, and smiling at Beauderriere, "we need a distraction if we are going to win this cursed, devilish, but strangely profitable war."

"I agree," said Lord Cardigan, as he packed another order for his cardigans, "we need to widen our market share; I have heard that the Russian general Count Knickerbocker, has taken over the nether garment and fancy ice cream markets at Sebastopol."

Lord Beauderriere looked around him at the other generals all nodding in agreement with Lord Cardigan.

"We must do something to stop this tide of profit leaving us," said the generals Marks and Spencer. Lord Beauderriere turned on them all.

"What in God's name are you all doing, we are here to protect our empire from foreign insurgents, and all you can bother about is your profit margins."

"If you've got an idea about how we should fight this war," said Raglan, "Have a go yourself, we are busy."

Lord Beauderriere stormed out of the tent and made his way to his brigade. He called his second-in-command to his tent.

"It seems that it is all down to us Petit Mort!" said Beauderriere.

"What is your plan, my friend?" replied Colonel Petit Mort. Beauderriere studied a map laid out on his table.

"We need to silence these guns at the end of this valley on the right," said Beauderriere, "they're not many and that will enable us to command the area."

Soon Beauderriere was astride his horse and leading his men in a charge. As they reached the mouth of the valley, Colonel Petit-Mort, galloped up the Beauderriere.

"My Lord, I have a feeling that we can beat them if we make this 45° turn to the left."

Well you can guess what happened, yes, into the valley of death and all that.

Beauderriere was one of the wounded and was taken to the field hospital. As he lay on his bed at night, he saw a lamp moving slowly towards him. It stopped at each bed until it reached him.

Holding the lamp was Florrie Nightjar, a lady of means who had taken it upon herself to come to the Crimea to tend the wounded. She leant over Beauderriere. "And how are you feeling my lord?" she said..

Beauderriere pulled himself up onto his elbow. "I think I am improving Madame, it was only a flesh wound."

The lady with the lamp looked at his legs and saw that they were both missing. "You are a very brave man and stupid."

AUTHORS NOTES ON THIS CHAPTER
I was going to call Florrie 'the lady with the limp', but then I'd have to give her a limp, and explain how she got it, and use it in a humorous way. I couldn't be arsed!

Chapter Twenty One
A Tomb With A View

Lord Henry Beauderriere threw down the morning paper in disgust. "Bloody, Carter, every bloody time, the bloody fu...!" Beauderriere's Aunt Clementine chose this moment top enter the breakfast room.

"Who's a bloody fu..., Henry?" she asked as she swept to the table and sat down.

"Oh, nothing Aunt, just thinking about...the flower show in the village, I expect that...Mrs Winterton will win again with her bloody fu...chsia, yes, fuchsia."

"Oh, I thought you were talking about that tosser Carter discovering another effing tomb," said Aunt, "if you are going to discover a tomb and bring me lots of jewels to compensate me for the thousands I have spent on you, since I took you in after your parents died on that big ship.."

"Titanic," said Beauderriere.

"I don't know how big it was, I just know it hit an ice cube and sank, as I was saying, after your parents died, I brought you up, educated you, launched your into society and you promised you would find me a tomb, didn't you"

"Yes Aunt," said Beauderriere, "I am planning to leave for Cairo in a couple of months, I found Uncle's old map in the attic, but I shall need some money for expenses etc. couple o'thousand should do."

Beauderriere viewed the mass of people from his seat atop a camel.

As he looked down on the throng milling around him, a policeman walked up.

"Oi, you!" shouted the policeman, "wot d'yer fink yer doing?"

Beauderriere took another swig from the bottle of Champagne he was carrying.

"I'm off to discover a Pharaoh's tomb!" he proudly announced.

"Well there ain't no bleedin' tombs in Oxford Street mush!" replied the policeman, "so sod off with that camel!"

Soon Beauderriere was on board ship heading for Egypt. He slowly moved along the deck, doffing his hat at the ladies and acknowledging the gentlemen with a nod of his head. The ship's First Officer brought him to a halt.

"Just to remind you my lord, we do not dress for dinner on the first night at sea," said the officer, "neither do we ride camels along the promenade deck."

With the camel stowed away, Beauderriere took his seat at the captain's table for dinner, it was the second time he had sat down as he had taken the First Officer's words literally and had arrived in the salon stark, bollock naked.

Upon his return, he received glaring looks of disgust from the gentlemen and admiring glances, and a few cabin numbers, from the ladies. After the first course, the conversation started and Beauderriere was the centre of attraction.

"Is this your first trip to Egypt my lord," said an army officer,

"Well, Major, it is actually my first trip in a ship; I haven't been able to, not since my parents were drowned in that big ship…"

"Titanic?" said the Major

"I suppose so," said Beauderriere "it was quite big anyway, all I know is that it hit an ice bucket and sank."

A few days later, Beauderriere was in Egypt. As he walked through the streets of Cairo, he took in the atmosphere, it was mostly camel shit. A man accosted him.

"You want naughty postcards?"

"No," replied Beauderriere.

"Genuine Persian carpet?"

"No," replied Beauderriere.

"Nice girl?"

"No," replied Beauderriere.

"Not so nice girl?"

"No," replied Beauderriere.

"You want nice boy!"

"No," replied Beauderriere.

"Not so nice b…"

"Look, I am looking for a guide named Abdul," said Beauderriere, "he lives on the Street of a Thousand Ar…"

"Artichokes?"

"No," replied Beauderriere.

"Artisans?"

"No," replied Beauderriere.

"Architects?"

"No," replied Beauderriere.

"Archaeologists?"

"No," replied Beauderriere, "Arseholes, I've had enough of this."

"Oh, the Street of a Thousand Arseholes, that's just down there on the left."

Beauderriere stared at the man, disgusted at the time wasted to do an old joke and walked away.

Before long, Beauderriere, his guide Abdul and an assorted collection of porters, workers and camels, were making their way across the trackless waste that was the desert. Every now and then, Beauderriere would consult his Uncle's map. They entered a valley and Abdul rode up to Beauderriere.

"This sir," said Abdul, "is the Valley of the Princes," Beauderriere and his companions rode on for about an hour and then made camp.

In his tent, Beauderriere and Abdul perused the map and Abdul pointed at a place at the foot of a large rock.

"I think, sir, that we should start our excavations here."

His men began digging and after a few days discovered a step, then another and another.

Soon Beauderriere was standing in front of a large doorway sealed with a cartouche. He turned to Abdul.

"What does this say, Abdul?"

"It says that this is the tomb of Prince Ramalangadingdong – hotep, he was a great Egyptian Prince sir, he was also a man of great wealth and not a little ingenuity. He was also a dabbler in the black arts and a magician of great repute."

"It says all that on this little seal?" said Beauderriere.

"No sir," said Abdul, "it says that in this leaflet, The Lost Tombs of Egypt."

"Does the cartouche say anything else?"

"Well, there is the prince's name and something else…it's in a very archaic form of hieroglyphic."

"Well, tell me roughly what it says, and I don't mean tell me in a rough manner, I mean just give me the gist of it."

"Umm, it seems that the prince is telling all desecraters of his tomb to piss off and leave him alone or he'll do you!" Beauderriere turned to Abdul.

"Pay off all the men and send they away, the less people know about this the better."

Beauderriere broke open the doorway and he made his way down a long dark corridor only illuminated by the flickering candle held by Abdul.

They saw many wondrous sights, piles of gold and gems. They reached the sarcophagus and began to remove the lid, as they did, there was a might crash in the corridor and it was blocked by many tons of rubble.

"Fuchsia," said Beauderriere, as the candle flickered and went out.

No more was heard from Lord Henry or Abdul. Legend has it that they are feasting with the gods, looked after by beautiful concubines and are living forever in the lap of luxury. Of course, we know that they slowly suffocated to death and are probably no more than skeletons.

AUTHORS NOTES ON THIS CHAPTER
Another well-written deeply researched chapter. As an historian I have endeavored to make sure that historical fact is kept true.

The Beauderrieres in Literature

And now we will delve into the Beauderriere Papers that mention our favourite family in Legend and Literature. As I mentioned in the introduction to this book, which you probably didn't read, a lot of fiction is based on the exploits of several members of the Beauderriere family. Here are some well-known stories that were inspired by our Beauderriere heroes.

I seems that Defoe, Conan Doyle, Baroness Orczy[1] et al all had access to the Beauderriere Papers and all of them, at the last moment, changed the characters names. Well, that's what I think anyway, who's to say I'm wrong, apart from anyone. Just read and enjoy!

---

[1] Look her up on the Internet if you don't know her!

Chapter Twenty Two
The Diary of Robinson Beauderriere or
Thank God It's Neville

HMS Agamemnon August 10th 1729 Ships Log as penned by Captain Harvey.

I am writing this unusual entry into the ships log so as to state my position upon our return to Portsmouth.

On the seventh day of August in the year 1729 in the reign of our most beloved king George the Second I was obliged by previous events and the entreaties of my crew to remove one Robinson Beauderriere from the vessel. Beauderriere was a continual drain on resources for which he refused to work for.

As ship's botanist it was his responsibility to tend the plants we had collected and to feed and take care of the fauna we had taken on board.

Dr. Beauderriere spent most of his time sitting on the fore-peak sleeping and ignoring his duties. He insisted on telling the steersman that he should steer the vessel 45° to the left and berated the coxswain about the latter's inability to keep the ship steady when he was shaving.

After discussing the problem with my junior officers it was decided to maroon him at sea. I have ordered the ship's doctor to write a report of the ejection verbatim to keep the record straight.

The Ejection of Dr. Robinson Beauderriere.

Robinson Beauderriere was manhandled off the ship and thrown into a leaky rowing boat with a few meagre rations. The captain leant over the side of the ship.

"I have had enough of your continual bleating about the hardship on this voyage, what did you expect you fool?" shouted the captain. Beauderriere stood up in the boat.

"This seat's wet, do you have a cloth?" he moaned.

The captain went and got a long pole and pushed Beauderriere's boat away from the side of the ship.

"Sod off you annoying twat, if you row for a couple of hours south west you will come to an uninhabited island and may the devil take you!" he shouted.

Following this harrowing, but successful event, the Captain plotted a new course and we made our way

The Diary of Robinson Beauderriere.

August 21st 1729

I am writing this diary in the hope that some brilliant and talented writer in the future will find this and tell my story.

After days of fighting the raging ocean, I came ashore on this desolate, uninhabited island. My little boat was wrecked on rocks, but I managed to salvage a few meagre possessions.

I decided that the first thing I needed to do was build a fire, luckily in my possessions was a flint and iron so I collected some dry grass and twigs and so after a few minutes had at least some warmth because the sun setting and it was getting colder. My next thought was food and water.

The food that was placed in the boat with me was sodden and inedible so I scoured the immediate area and found some fruit that looked as if it would suffice. I ate it all with relish, I was lucky to find some gentleman's relish amongst my meagre possessions.[2]

I awoke in the early with terrible stomach pains, obviously the fruit or the relish was a bit off. As I lay there moaning and befouling the immediate area, I heard a noise in the bushes. I thought it must be some wild animal attracted by my malodorous emissions.

---

[2] Can we please assume that anything I use was among my possessions or this chapter will go on and on about me finding or making them. Thank you.

In the dim light, through half closed eyes I saw a figure creeping towards me. I assumed that my end was nigh and that death is much better that the pain and the stench I was producing. I passed out.

I awoke the next morning to find that I was sitting in a large cauldron of water with a fire underneath and a group of natives dancing, chanting and throwing various vegetable into the pot with me. I panicked, I was among cannibals, I was going to provide them with a nutritious meal, something I hadn't managed to have.

The water was warm, not too hot and as I waited for death to engulf me and native came over to the pot, dipped his finger in and tasted it.

"Nearly ready old chum." he said in a cut glass English accent, "how are you feeling now?"

"Er, fine, thank you, when are you going to eat me?" I said nervously. He looked at me aghast.

"Bloody typical, I go out of my way to save you and to cure you of the malady you have and you accuse me of wanting to eat you!" said the native. He turned to his companions.

"He thinks we're going to eat him, he thinks we're cannibals!" he called to them. The natives stopped dancing and walked over to the cauldron.

"Bloody cheek I say, just because we put him in the Curing Pot and added some healing herbs he thinks were uncivilised!" said the other native.

"But it's not just herbs, there's carrots and onions in here!" bemoaned Beauderriere.

The native turned to a rather fat native who was sneaking away from the group.

"Sebastian, did you put these vegetables in the Curing Pot?" said the first native. The fat native slunk back to the group.

"Sorry Neville, nobody told me we were curing him, I thought we had decided to go back to the old ways!" said Sebastian.

"Shame on you Seb, for what you've done there will be no Sherry trifle for you tonight!" He turned to Beauderriere.

"Sorry about that Mr....?"

"Beauderriere." replied Robinson.

"Mr Beauderriere," said the first native, "my name is Neville, please accept our apologies, we put you in the pot to curing you of the poisonous fruit you ate and to mask the eye-watering stink that was coming from you. Allow me to help you out."

Soon they were all sitting down for an evening meal of pork and all sorts of tasty things. Sebastian the native was sitting apart from the others looking rather forlorn. Robinson picked up a coconut shell, put some trifle in it and handed it to Sebastian.

Sebastian looked at Neville who nodded his agreement and then started to eat the trifle.

"All friends now? said Robinson. The group smiled.

"Tell me Neville, how is it that you can all speak impeccable English yet live on this desert island thousands of miles from anywhere?"

"Missionaries, they came to the island years ago, built schools and hospitals and taught us the English language. said Neville "after they had taught us all they knew and had imparted some sort of civilized way upon us, making us dress, be polite to strangers, help people when you can.....we ate them!" Beauderriere stood up and took a step back.

"We don't do that anymore, although as you noticed with Seb, some still think back to the old days." said Neville, "we'll make you some clothes suitable for the island and teach you how to hunt and trap animals and as soon as we spy a ship we will signal it for you."

The weeks turned into months and the months turned into years and after about three years a call of 'Ship Ahoy' was made and a signal fire was lit.

Soon a rowing boat was sighted coming out of a large sailing ship and when it beached on the sand Robinson collected his belongings and walk to the boat with Neville and Neville.

"Good morning Captain, we have a passenger for you, please meet Robinson Beauderriere!" said Neville. The Captain looked at Robinson.

"Oh No, you of all people, I thought you would have perished, you useless great lump of….."

"No Captain Harvey, I've changed, I have learned to do things and to help others!"

"Well if that is so, you are welcome back on the Agamemnon!" said the captain.

Robinson and the sailors said their goodbyes and loaded the good fruit and water supplied by the islanders and rowed back to the Agamemnon.

After a few days, Robinson stopped being so helpful and resumed his place in the fore-peak and dozed off.

"Keep it steady steersman, you're spilling my tea!! called out Beauderriere.

The captain shook his head and mentioned to the boatswain that her should look out for another island to dump Beauderriere on as soon as possible.

AUTHORS NOTES ON THIS CHAPTER
The story of Robinson Crusoe was supposed to be based on Alexander Selkirk, but we know different, don't we!

Chapter Twenty Three
They Seek Him Here

Sir Percy Beauderriere was a typical aristocrat of the eighteenth century. He spent his days hunting and his nights dancing and playing cards.

He and his boon companion, Lord Bairley-Saine, had a secret that was imperative to keep to themselves. Sir Percy was none other than *The Scarlet Foreskin*, the notorious nemesis of the French Revolution. *The Scarlet Foreskin* would use daring ploys to seize the heads of the French aristocracy from the embrace of Madame Guillotine.

Why does he call himself *The Scarlet Foreskin*, it is because there was no one to save him from the embrace of Madame Fifi, the famous courtesan and disease carrier.

Sir Percy was holding a ball. (I was very tempted to do a testicle joke here, but resisted it.) He had invited all the French aristos he had saved. He stood at the door as they were introduced.

"My lords ladies and gentlemen, The Duc de Grande Tete," called the butler, "and the Duchesse."

This went on for a while; in fact, Sir Percy had almost lost interest until he heard his Butler intone.

"His Excellency, Monsieur Shoveitalong, of the French Committee for Peace," intoned the butler. See I told you he intoned it! The Frenchman moved over to Sir Percy with his hand extended.

"You must excuse your servant, Sir Percy; my name is Chauvetelan of the French Security Force."

"Welcome to my humble home," said Sir Percy, "Monsieur Shoveitin, may I introduce to you my closest friend and supporter, Lord Bairley-Saine."

The gentlemen all bowed graciously at one another. Chauvetelan drew Sir Percy to one side.

"I feel that I have to confide in you Sir Percy," began Chauvetelan, "as a man who has many connections among both the English and French aristocracy. I desperately need to get my hands on the Foreskin." Sir Percy looked at him askance. "Well, Monsieur," said Sir Percy, "you don't beat about the bush do you." Sir Percy took the Frenchman by the arm and led him into a rose arbour. The Frenchman began to protest.

"Please, Sir Percy that is not what I meant" They took a turn around the garden.

"This Scarlet Foreskin has been nothing but trouble and embarrassment to the whole of New Regime," said Chauvetelan. Sir Percy coughed quietly into his handkerchief.

"He is," continued the Frenchman, "a perpetual thorn in our side. He takes the accursed aristos from the blade of the guillotine and whisks them away to who knows where." In the distance came be heard the butler.

"The Count and Countess of Sacre Bleu, the Marquis de Mange-Tout and other assorted French aristocrats, with strange names, newly arrived from the blade of the guillotine."

"Well, I don't see how I can be of use to you." inquired Sir Percy.

"Just keep your ear to the ground and inform me of anything you may hear," said Chauvetelan. "I will have the Foreskin in my hand, I know, before long."

"To each his own, Monsieur, come we must meet my guests."

Our story now moves to the bustling city of Paris. Everyone was wearing the red cap of liberty.

Seated outside an inn are three dirty looking individuals, obviously up to know good, and talking in whispers.

"It's no good Sir Percy, you're going to have to speak up," said Lord Bairley-Saine, "I can't hear a word you're saying." One of the other men clamped his hand over Bairley-Saine's mouth.

"Keep your voice down," whispered Sir Percy, "we have a job to do and we mustn't get caught."

"What's the job this time?" said the third man, Sir Percy's butler.

"We are to rescue the Countess de Belle Gauloises, reputed to be the most beautiful woman in France. She is due to go to the guillotine today at noon."

"What is your plan sir," asked the butler as he served them tea.

"We shall sneak in to the Bastille," said Sir Percy, "locate the Countess. I shall then disguise myself as the Countess, and take the journey to the guillotine. You will take the Countess back to the ship and then return to assist my escape."

Nothing more was heard of Sir Percy Beauderriere or the Scarlet Foreskin. The Countess was safely delivered to the ship and when Lord Bairley-Saine and the butler returned to help Sir Percy's escape a soldier told them that the time for the executions were brought forward an hour.

Bairely-Saine and the butler cursed themselves for not returning straight away, but as they thought the executions were not happening until noon, they thought that they deserved a spot of brunch.

"So, the Countess de Belle Gauloises has been executed then," said Lord Bairley-Saine.

The soldier smiled to himself.

"Yes, she went to the guillotine rather strangely. She kept looking over her shoulder and muttering something about stuffing the barely sane or something like that. I'll tell you what though," continued the soldier, "some say she was the most beautiful woman in France, but I could swear she had a five o'clock shadow, and her language was not what you expect from a French aristo. Bugger this, bleeding that, I'll rip his bloody bollocks off."

So Lord Bairley-Saine and the butler made their way to the docks and sailed home happy in the knowledge that they were not going to go on any more adventures.

They looked up at the wheelhouse and thought they saw the ghost of Sir Percy wearing a dress and holding his head on with one hand.

When the ship was in open water, the ship took a 45° turn to the left, and they were never seen again.

AUTHORS NOTES ON THIS CHAPTER
I am also quite pleased with this chapter. I am not saying I am displeased with others, just that I'm pleased with this one. Thank you.

Chapter Twenty Four
Elementary My Dear Beauderriere

It is late summer 1888 and Dr. John H Wilson returned from abroad and decided to look for an apartment in London where he could set up his medical practice. Everything was so expensive so he decided to find someone to share the apartment.

As he walked through Regent Street on his way to Baker Street where he had heard of an apartment to rent when he was accosted by what appeared to be a bent old beggar.

"A penny for an old soldier what 'as done his duty to Queen and Country kind sir?

Wilson stopped and put his hand into his pocket and produced a whistle.

"Clear off, you filthy disreputable parasite, or I will summon a constable." He put the whistle to his lips.

The beggar seemed to visibly change before his eyes. The next moment, standing next to him was a well-dressed gentleman of means.

"I say," said the gentleman, "I have never seen such vehemence before, especially when I see that you were a Army Surgeon and that you have just returned from Afghanistan where you would have been plagued by street beggars"

"What makes you say that?" said Wilson."

"It is my hobby, I can tell you were an Army Surgeon because you are still wearing your blood soaked apron and that you have a tan, hence an Army Surgeon with a tan, must have returned from the Afghan wars, which would not have happened if the Government had listened to me." The gentleman pouted and looked at his fingernails.

"Am I right?" he enquired looked at him with his penetrating eyes.

"You're right about the apron and Afghanistan," said Wilson.

"I thought as much," said the gentleman, "I have a distinct aptitude for knowing these things."

"The apron is blood-stained because I work three days a week in my local Afghan butchers and I have not had to chance to change it," said Wilson.

"Oh," said the gentleman. Wilson continued, "and the tan is there because I have just returned from holidaying in the South of France."

"I see," said the gentleman.

"So your distinct aptitude is really a load of old bollocks really."

"What do you mean, I got blood-stained apron and Afghanistan right," said the gentleman, "anyway, I must be off, I have an apartment to see in Baker Street, although I fear I will not be able to afford it on my own."

"Not number 221b Baker Street," asked Wilson.

"They very same," replied the gentleman.

"I am on my way there myself," said Wilson, "and I am in the same predicament as you, not being sure I will be able to afford it."

"Well, well, perhaps we can afford it together if it is suitable for both our needs, my name is Beauderriere Holmes."

"I'm Dr. Wilson, pleased to meet you."

"Likewise," said Holmes, "Oh, about our earlier discussion, you couldn't let me have a penny could you, I'm dying for a piss."

Soon the two were making their way to Baker Street. They stopped outside number 221b and rang the bell. They heard the stomping of heavy feet and the jangling of chains and locks. Suddenly a voice cried out.

"I hope you haven't come here to rape and ravish me, have you?" said the voice behind the door.

"I haven't," said Holmes "but I'm not so sure about Wilson.

The clanking continued and the door slowly opened. Beauderriere quickly removed his blood-stained apron lest its presence disturbs the landlady.

"What do you want?" warbled the landlady.

"We've come to see about the apartment you have to let," said Holmes with an air of authority.

"It's gorn," said the landlady

"What do you mean it's gorn," demanded Holmes.

"I'm using the local patois of the area, when I say 'gorn' I mean 'gone'. I've let it to two gentlemen," said the landlady, "one's a consulting detective, and the other is a doctor, that's what I mean when I say it's gone...gorn!" The landlady then shut the door quickly.

Wilson turned to Holmes, who was trying to release his coat tails that had been caught in the door.

"Well, that's a fine kettle of fish, what do we do now?" Holmes was still tugging at his coat tails when the door opened again. Holmes flew across the pavement and landed in a pile of horse shit. The landlady poked her head out.

"My sister in Whitechapel has some rooms to let, you may be lucky there," said the landlady and handed Wilson a piece of paper with the name address on it.

They flagged down a cab and they made their way to the East End. The cabbie stopped at the top of the street and opened the doors.

"This is as far as I go gentlemen," he said, "don't like this area, funny goings on and that." Wilson paid the cabbie and he and Holmes made their cautious way down the street.

"This is it," said Wilson, "Number 13."

They knocked and the door was opened by a slightly older version of the Baker Street landlady.

"We understand from your sister," began Holmes, "that you have rooms to let, is that true."

"I have indeed gentlemen, would you like to inspect them. The rent is very popular, two guineas a week."

"I don't think that two guineas a week rent would be very popular," said Wilson.

"It's very popular with me sir." Holmes and Wilson entered the house, the rooms are found to be satisfactory, and after an hour and a half of haggling, the rent was agreed at two and a half guineas a week.

The pair soon settled down to a routine, Wilson carried on his work at the Afghan butchers and when he was not working, he would stand on street corners jeering at beggars. Holmes, on the other hand, seemed very different from before.

He would stand at the window and stare for hours at the passers-by. At night, he would go out and not return until the early hours. When he returned his was covered with blood.

After a couple of weeks, whilst sitting at breakfast, Wilson noticed an article in the paper, which he ventured to read aloud to Holmes.

"'Another Dreadful Murder in Whitechapel. Local prostitute found dead. Horribly mutilated.'" said Wilson, "what do you make of that Holmes, some maniac no doubt."

At that moment there was a knock on the door and Inspector Lestrange of Scotland Yard entered.

"Not necessarily a maniac Wilson" began Holmes, "it may well be the work of a scientist, or anatomist."

"What makes you say that," asks Wilson.

"You must never assume," said Holmes, "that someone who can cause such bestial mutilation must be a lunatic." Lestrange sat down in the proffered chair and smiled.

"So, you are discussing the Whitechapel Murders, Mr Holmes." he said.

"Yes, Lestrange, have you made any progress with them?" Holmes asked.

"No, nothing, we are completely baffled, that is why I have called on you." said an embarrassed Lestrange.

"What must we look for then Holmes," asked Wilson.

Holmes stood and began to pace the room. He lit his pipe and started on his deductions.

"First," he began, "we must look to a man with solitary vices."

"Like you," exclaimed Wilson.

"What do you mean?" asked Holmes.

"Well," said Wilson, "I've seen you many a time going into the water closet with a copy of the Illustrated Police News, and some strange sounds coming from inside."

"Yes, well," mumbled Holmes, "next we must look for a man, for I am convinced this miscreant is a man, who has an utter dislike for women."

"Like you," exclaimed Wilson.

"What do you mean?" asked Holmes.

"Well," said Wilson, "you never seem to have a woman companion and seem to prefer to spend your time in the Turkish baths volunteering to give the other clients massages."

"Yes, well," mumbled Holmes, "next we must look for a man who goes out late at night and returns home exhausted and covered in blood."

"Like you," exclaimed Wilson.

"What do you mean?" asked Holmes.

"Well," said Wilson, "you go out late at night and come back covered in blood."

"Of course I do," fumed Holmes, "I have to do your late night stint at the Afghan butchers, you prick."

"Oh, of course," said Wilson, "well I do have this other part-time position that seems to take up my time." Holmes turned to Lestrange.

"It seems we are both at an impasse Inspector." Later that day, Holmes put on his butchers apron and left the house to go to his butcher's job, Wilson carefully place some sharpened knives into his black bag and closed the bag with a snap.

He put on his evening clothes and his top hat and threw a black cape around his shoulders. He left his rooms and made his way downstairs.

As he reached the bottom of the stairs, the landlady popped her head out of her room.

"You off out again Doctor, she enquired, "more good deeds to do in the East End no doubt."

"No doubt Mrs Hudson," said Wilson, "no doubt at all. He then gave a maniacal laugh and left the house.

AUTHORS NOTES ON THIS CHAPTER
Another brilliant chapter, brilliantly written. I often wonder where all these brilliant ideas come from!

Chapter Twenty Five
Robin Beauderriere
and His Not So Merry Men

We all know the story of Robin Hood and his Merry Men and their escapades in Nottingham and Sherwood Forest. The Beauderriere history tells us of another Robin who lived in another forest.

It is morning in the Greenwood, the birds are singing and the sun is shining. Nature heralds the new day. Robin Beauderriere wakes from his slumber, rises, stretches and piddles up against a gnarled old oak.

Unfortunately, sleeping under this gnarled old oak is Friar Pleat, Robin Beauderriere's gnarled old spiritual advisor.

"Why don't you bugger off!" moaned Friar Pleat. Robin always ignored this sort of advice and took a deep breath.

"Methinks, dear Friar Pleat," said Beauderriere, "that we are most fortunate to live in such a pleasant place."

Beauderriere put his hunting horn to his lips and blew. The sound reverberated through the trees. His faithful band of outlaws began to stir.

"What arsehole is blowing is horn at this time of the morning?" asked Little Tom, in a not unthreatening manner.

"'Tis I, Little Tom, 'tis I who have the horn," said Beauderriere. "I, your fearless leader."

Beauderriere stood with his arms akimbo surveying his men.

"Tis a fine day today, a fine enough day to teach that Sheriff of Nottingham a thing or two, what do you say?"

"I say, sod off fearless leader or I'll cut your bollocks off," said Little Tom through gritted teeth.

Beauderriere ignored Little Tom's threat and strutted around rousing his men for the day ahead.

"As soon as we have broken our fast, we will ride into Nottingham and rescue the fair damsel the Lady Margaret," said Beauderriere.

Another of Beauderriere's fearless outlaws, Will Cerise roused himself and stood up.

"Well Robin, love, there is a tiny little problemo in doing that," said Will.

"And, my friend, what is the problem in going to Nottingham and rescuing the Lady Margaret, where's the problem with that?"

"Well, sweet chucks," said Will, "Nottingham is hundreds of miles away, we live in the New Forest, not Sherwood, and as for the Lady Margaret, being built like a brick shithouse, whatever bricks are, so she is perfectly capable of looking after herself."

"We have to do something," said Robin, "we're outlaws, brigands, ne'r-do-well's; we can't just sit around all day doing nothing."

Will walked over to Robin and put his arm around his shoulders.

"We do a fair bit of outlawing," said Will encouragingly, "only last week we pinched some apples from Sir Randolph's orchard, didn't we."

"I am Robin Beauderriere, scion of a great dynasty. I can't go down in history as Robin the Pippin Pincher, "not only that," he continued, "we've got to get some money and give it to the poor."

Little Tom stood up stretched and walked over to the gnarled old oak and pissed over the gnarled old Friar.

"Stuff the poor, we need to get some money and keep it ourselves," said Tom, "I'm not going to spend the rest of my days in this forest, freezing my arse off and living only on a diet of apples and whatever small mammal we can catch."

Friar Pleat stood up and wiped the piddle from his tonsure.

"I agree with Little Tom," he began, "I joined this miserable band because I believed it would lead to untold riches and piles of food, something has to be done." The whole band of outlaws agreed.

"What do you suggest we do Friar," asked Robin, "ride to Sir Randolph's castle and steal all the gold from his treasury?"

"What a good idea," said Little Tom, "let's get going, I could do with a good fight."

"I was only joking," remonstrated Robin, "his castle is heavily fortified, he has men-at-arms, we could get hurt. If we're caught, they will do unspeakable things to us, strip us naked and abuse us!"

Will picked up his sword and bow and walked up to Little Tom. "Well, that's got my vote Little Tom, stripped naked you say Robin, what are we waiting for!"

Soon all the outlaws and their reluctant leader were on their way to Sir Randolph's castle. They had put on the habits of monks and arrived at the castle chanting. A burly Sergeant-at-Arms stopped them at the gate.

"Halt, who are you and what's your business here," said the Sergeant.

The outlaws all wearing their cowls turned to Friar Pleat. He made his way through the outlaws and stood to face the Sergeant.

"Well my good man," he began, "may God and his angels bless you and your family."

"I ain't got no bloody family," said the Sergeant, "what do you want!"

"We have come to the castle," said Friar Pleat, "to celebrate the Feast of St. Peregrine the Pious."

The Sergeant walked through the outlaws and noticed the shoes that Will Cerise was wearing.

"Why is this monk wearing these delicate and fancy shoes," he said, "I thought monks were supposed to live a life of penury." Friar Pleat walked over to the Sergeant and led him away.

"He's wearing them for a penance; he had an unclean thought, and must wear them to show that he is repentant."

"Umm, they suit him though," said the Sergeant, "Anyway, I ain't never heard of this St. Peregrine the Pissarse, who was he?"

"St. Peregrine the Pious was a man who worshipped God in his own way," began Friar Pleat, "he would spend days in brothels doing his best to convert the harlots to Christianity. He would show them many ways to love God."

"I bet he did!" said the Sergeant, "anyway, the chapel is over there, next to the treasury. I shall look forward to hearing more about this St Peregrine the Poser."

"The Pious," said Friar Pleat over his shoulder as the monks quickly made their way to the chapel.

"Whatever," said the Sergeant as he went off to resume his duties.

The outlaws entered the chapel and began to make their plans.

"What luck," said Will, "right next to the treasury. How are we going to get inside?

"We could smash down the wall," said Little Tom. "and grab the treasure and run very fast to the castle entrance and escape."

"That is one idea Tom, and a very good idea too," said Robin, "but I fear it would end with us all dead, we don't know what sort of treasure it is, it could be coins or jewels, or bloody great lumps of gold. We need to have a look at first."

"Well," said Will, "how are we going to do that, walk up to Sir Randolph as ask him to let us have a look at the treasure."

"Exactly," said Robin, "exactly."

Soon Robin, Will, Little Tom and Friar Pleat, were standing in the august presence of Sir Randolph de Villainous.

"My Sergeant-at Arms," began Sir Randolph, "informs me that you need to bless my treasure as part of the Feast of St Peregrine the Pompous."

"The Pious," said Friar Pleat.

"Whatever, why do you need to see my treasure, surely earthly wealth is an anathema to you"

"Well, yes, my lord," said Friar Pleat, "but St Peregrine, although a poor man, had the ability, through prayer, to increase the wealth of others."

"Did he now, what needs to be done?"

Robin stepped forward at this point.

"We will need to spend one night alone with the treasure, a night of prayer, but before that we will need to have a lot of food and wine, as decreed by St Peregrine the Whatever." At this point Sir Randolph noticed Will's shoes

"I say, they're very nice, where did you get them?" Will stepped forward and showed the shoes to Sir Randolph.

"I have a little man in the next town," said Will, "who, apart from his other little talents, is an absolute dream at cobbling,"

"You must give me his name," said Sir Randolph.

Little Tom grabbed hold of Will and wrenched the shoes off his feet and handed them to Sir Randolph.

"Perhaps you will accept them as a gift," said Tom, "now that his penance is through."

"Thank you," said Sir Randolph, "return in one hour and we will feast you."

As they trooped back to the chapel, Will turned on Little Tom.

"Why did you give him my lovely shoes?"

"They were getting to be a bloody liability," said Tom, "why can't you wear shoes like us, they're perfectly suitable."

"I like those shoes, cost me a fortune," said Will.

"All they cost you," began Robin, "was a blow-job for the cobbler, now come on, we have plans to make."

The outlaws spent the night making sacks out of two of the outlaw's habits. The next morning they walked out of the chapel and stood outside the treasury.

The Sergeant-at-Arms opened the treasury door for them, they went in, and the door was closed behind them.

The outlaws stood staring at the piles of chests and boxes. While some of the outlaw's chanted prayers, the rest began to fill the sacks.

After a while, Will turned to Robin. "I've just had a thought," he said.

"If it's about how this treasure house would look better with velvet hangings and a nice rush floor forget it," snapped Robin.

"No!" said Will, looking around the place, "well, maybe, but it's not that."

"What then?" asked Robin.

"If we take all this treasure," began Will, "they will soon know it's gone because they'll check it when we leave and come after us."

Robin smiled and drew Will over to the other side of the treasury.

"I've already thought of that," whispered Robin, "Didn't you wonder why I brought along Tiny Much and Teeny Mick?"

"You mean those two very tiny people we used to climb the apple trees?"

"Yes," said Robin

Soon everything was ready and the two large chests were emptied. Robin casually walked over to Tiny and Teeny, went behind them, and hit them over the head, knocking them unconscious.

He picked them both up and put one in each chest and scattered some of the treasure over them to make it look as if the chests were full. As soon as this was done, there was a loud knocking at the treasury door.

"Its morning," said the Sergeant's voice, "time to come out."

The outlaws left the room and made their way to the Great Hall. Sir Randolph greeted them warmly.

"My holy friends, welcome back, how's the treasure, doubled it yet?"

Robin moved forward and handed Sir Randolph a piece of parchment.

"Read that when we've gone, not before or it will not work," said Robin, "and now we must leave the castle to go to Canterbury to celebrate the feast of St. Adidas the Speedy."

The outlaws moved of very quickly and soon were out of the castle and on their way back to the forest. Sir Randolph opened the parchment and written on it were the words:

Dear Sir Randolph, if you wish to double your money, put it all on the favourite in the 3 o'clock. Robin Beauderriere.

What Sir Randolph did next is not known, what Robin did is documented, he and his outlaws went on holiday to Sherwood Forest and were never heard of again.

AUTHORS NOTES ON THIS CHAPTER
Apparently Lincoln Green wasn't actually green. It was a corruption of Lincoln Graine, which is a scarlet colour. Bright red, perfect for hiding in the greenwood...NOT!

Chapter Twenty Six
The Beauderriere Extended Family

Sebastian Beauderriere

Not all Beauderrieres made their mark on history. Quite a lot of them excelled and I use that word quite wrongly, in other areas more cerebral. Read on!

Our first 'intellectual' Beauderriere is **Sebastian 'Cosmic' Beauderriere**, a self-styled spiritualist, and cryptozoologist. He has spent many years searching out the mysteries of the world. His only failing is his naivety. Here are a few of items from his journal.

The Loch Ness Monster It's Real!

I thought that a couple of days camping at Loch Ness would be beneficial to my health and perhaps I could do a little investigation on the Monster. There was a tapping on my tent, so I got out and saw a man in a kilt standing near my camp.

"Good-day to you sir," said the man, and then he went on to ask me if I was up there for the 'beastie'. I replied that I was actually on holiday. He introduced himself as Hamilton McCurdle and that he had seen the Monster over 1000 times. I offered him a cup of tea but he refused and took a can of Special Brew out of his sporran. I asked him about the Loch Ness Monster, what did it look like?

"Och, it's a strange looking beastie. Not as big as you would think, but a moonster all the same." I asked this very intelligent man, what sort of size is it.

"It's aboot as big as a log, in fact, out of the 1000 sightings I expect it was a log aboot 999 times.!" I was caught up in the magic of this.

"So the monster is some gigantic primeval log that haunts the loch?" He looked at me, at least I think he did as his eyes were obscured by the thick lenses of his spectacles.

"I didna say it was gigantic, I said it was a big as a log." This made me think. As we sat there musing on this another kilted gentleman walked up.

"Good morning to you Hamilton, and to you stranger." Mr McCurdle stood up, swayed a bit, and replied, "Good morning to you, Hector."

I said my good mornings and offered Hector a cup of tea, which he declined in favour of a can of Special Brew from Mr McCurdle's sporran.

"So, you've come to see the 'beastie'?" said Hector. I explained that I was on holiday and was interested in the Monster. "I've seen it y'ken," said Hector. I was most fortunate to meet two locals who had intimate knowledge of the monster.

"I was coming oot a the pub late one night, and got inta me boot to go across to me cottage. Aboot half across, och, me knees still tremble at the thought of it, right in front of me this thing reared up in front me boot!"

I was all agog, at last a first encounter sighting from some who knows the loch like the back of his hand. I asked him to go on, but he seemed to be looking at the back of his hand mystified. I asked Hector to go one.

"Gone on aboot what?" he asked. "What was it you saw in the loch."

"Ah, the beastie y'mean, ay, there is was still on the water, looking at me with its dark eye, it was magical!" "What did it look like?" I enquired.

"Looked like, a bloody great log, that's what it looked like, not gigantic mind you, but big, I turned and rowed for the bank, I didn't what to meet it again."

The two men sauntered off fortified by the Special Brew and the ten pound note I had given them each. I came away from Loch Ness confident in the knowledge that I had met two remarkable men who, in their wisdom, tried to deflect my enquiries, but only convinced me that there was something unknown in the deep waters of Loch Ness, not gigantic, but unknown.

Born Again Has-Beans

When the face of the Virgin Mary was found in a tin of beans a new religion was born. Now Haricotists from all over the world gather to communicate and eat the 'fruit of the Lord' (*their terms for canned haricots in tomato sauce*).

I recently went to a Haricotist communion and was surprised to meet many completely normal people there. Archie Worrell, who founded the movement, is an ex-Raelist who says he admires Reverend Moon and now models himself on L Ron Hubbard explains how he saw the light.

"I was just reading 'A Course on Miracles' backwards when I had the sudden urge to open a tin of beans and look inside, it was bizarre," explained Archie, "because I totally against eating food of any kind."

Does Archie believe that God told him to open the beans?

"Oh most certainly, I told my psychiatrist about it and even he was slightly wary when I said I'd decided to stop taking my schizophrenia tablets and become a Haricotist."

At the Haricotist communion I notice that music is central to worship, all Haricotists play wind instruments and there is an unearthly aroma surrounding the congregation.

"That's the Holy Spirit presenting itself as a tangible, almost edible fragrance." explained another totally normal follower, a middle-aged fan of Alistair Crowley who lives in a gazebo in the Outer Hebrides.

"There are many varieties of aroma and I've smelt them all." said Norman, yet another completely ordinary and sound-minded person. Norman, who is dressed as The Starship

Enterprise when I meet him, confesses that he used to be unstable.

"I honestly believed I was a Dalek," he laughs, "but now I realise that's just ridiculous."

Since conducting this interview Archie Worrell has starved to death. He was cremated in the Haricotist tradition, his ashes were mixed with some soggy chipolatas and canned.

Weird Creatures

Forget the Beast of Bodmin Moor. Don't even think about the Phoenix or Puff the Magic Dragon. Erase all knowledge of the Jabberwocky and every other mythical creature. They are but nothing when compared to the outlandish beasts that roam the peaceful pastures of this green and pleasant land.

I went to meet Hector Hockett, a pig-swill sorter from Hertfordshire who was amongst the first to spot what is being called a Demi-Gonk in a barn not far from his home.

"I was completely stunned," says Hector, who was recently released into the community, "the creature had the head and body of a human but the facial features, hair and demeanour of a Gonk."

Mrs Betty Oates, another local who is recovering from a lobotomy when I meet her, reports.

"I first saw the Demi-Gonk last month. I'd just come out of hospital the day I saw it. It walked into my garden carrying a can of Special Brew, growled at me and then slunk off behind the potting shed. We think it's been eating the chickens."

So, is there any evidence to suggest that Demi-Gonks actually exist? Luckily another local person was able to capture an image of a Demi-Gonk on camera.

"It just stood there, swaying and it seemed quite happy to pose for a photo, a photo that didn't come out!. I couldn't believe it." says Wilf Citanul. "The strange thing was that I didn't feel afraid. At first I thought it was my daughter-in-law who is a strippagram, then I realised it was fully clothed and had a better figure than her."

With such sound testimonies from so many reliable witnesses I can only conclude that Demi-Gonks really do exist.

Crop Circles

It was midnight when I arrived outside the sleepy village of Lower Undercarriage. Across the wide expanse of cornfields I could see flashing lights and I could hear faint, unearthly noises. I ventured nearer and stumbled across someone else interested it what was obviously, the making of crop circles by beings not of this world.

"Look where yer bleedin' going, yer big tit!' said my new companion. I had evidently taken him by surprise. I introduced myself and refused a swig from his can of Special Brew. I asked him if he had seen the being that were causing the crop circles. "Yes," he said, "it's them bleedin' tossers from the next vi…"

"Galaxy!" I interrupted.

"If yer like," he said and mumbled something about one being born every minute, This man was a fount of knowledge, not only did he know the home galaxy of these beings, he also knew the gestation period of its females.

We watched the flashing light and listened to the strange noises for another thirty minutes and then everything went dark and quiet. A little while later we both stood up and my companion, who seemed a little unsteady on his feet, collapsed to the ground again. I left him and made my way to the site of the crop circles.

The ground was covered with strange geometric shapes and the whole area had a strange unearthly aroma. I took photographs and walked back to my companion. With him were three other people, all rather unsteady on their feet, but generous enough to offer me swigs from their Special Brew cans and to tell me that I was their best mate. Such is the camaraderie amongst those whose minds are on a higher plane.

I offered them a lift into the village which they gladly accepted. They were a jovial bunch, each time my friend mumbled something to them, they all burst out laughing and pointing at me. We stopped in the village and my passengers all got out, they moved off fortified by their beer and the £20 note I had given them.

Next morning I found the rear seats of my caravanette covered with corn ears and straw and I could detect the faint aroma I had smelt in the cornfield.

The man at the valet cleaning company said the smell was a combination of piss and vomit, I think not. I believe that I had an encounter with beings from a galaxy far, far away.

Invisibility

Whilst sitting at the breakfast table I read a letter that made me put my egg spoon down in surprise. The letter was from a friend of mine, Dicken Dalrymple. The missive informed me that strange goings on were happening in the tiny village of Lower Undercarriage in Cornwall.

This revelation was no surprise to me because I have investigated many a phenomena in this village. It seems to me that Lower Undercarriage must be a cosmic crossroads of the universe. I motored down the following day. I parked my caravanette in the pub carpark and made my way into the village. The whole place was deserted, yet I had the feeling that I was being watched.

As I walked through the village I came across Dicken Dalrymple half in and half out of a horse trough. If the trough had been full of water, he might have drowned and the world would have lost one of its greatest mystics.

I pulled him upright and sat him down on a nearby bench, as he seemed unsteady on his feet. I offered his a sip of diluted fruit juice from my vacuum flask, but he seemed to prefer a swig from his can of Special Brew. He looked up at me and said,

"They've all gone, yet, somehow, they're still here. They're invisible!"

I looked around and he was right, the place was devoid of people, but as I scanned the area I could see the odd twitching of curtains and sudden closing of doors. I turned to Dicken.

"When did this all start?" He took another swig from his can.

"Last night there was a fog," he began. I thought to myself that this was classic, fog, disappearances'. He continued.

"Just after the pub shut, I wandered through the village, just me and my shotgun. In the murky shadows I saw strange misshapen figures. It was obvious to me that beings from another world have used the fog as cover for an invasion. I started to shout at them and started shooting into dark corners where I thought I saw them cowering.

The villagers ran around screaming and shouting something about an armed madman and then they…disappeared. They've all gone to another dimension, yet, somehow, they're still here."

I patted him on the shoulder, placed a £20 note in his top pocket, turned, and made my way out of the village. I left behind a mystery that may never be solved.

Like many of his family, Sebastian also worked as Spiritual Guide for Clackhorne's Magazine. He also did a Hollywood Interview.

Hollywood Interviews

Each Month one of our Columnists will interview a famous Hollywood Star. This month **Sebastian 'Cosmic' Beauderriere** talks to:

Luigi Carbone, director of such films as 'The Mind Blower'; 'The Thing Under the Bed' and 'Telepathic Man'

Sebastian: Welcome, if I could ask you, did you know how influential your films would be to believers such as me?

Luigi: Wotta you talk about, itsa just a films, a way to maka da big money froma da morons lika you!

Sebastian: What perception!. you must have some sort of sixth sense..when did you realise this?

Luigi: Wotsa all this talking sixth sense bollocks...sixth sense, I thinka you hava no bleeding sense..ask me about my films you stupido!

Sebastian: I don't believe it.. fantastic, that's why I'm here.. to ask you about your films, how did you know.. Unbelievable!

Sebastian drops his notes on the floor and he crawls on his hands and knees to pick them up.

Luigi: I am a not going to sit here wiv this bleeding looney!

At this point Luigi Carbone left the room. Sebastian returns to his chair and see Luigi's chair empty.

Sebastian: He's dematerialised himself, that was brilliant, I can honestly say that I have met of the foremost Masters of the Occult. Brilliant.

Suddenly all the lights go out.

Sebastian: I knew that would happen...brilliant!

Sebastian was eventually found a quiet room in a cosy seaside boarding house where he spends his days writing and scratching his bollocks.

Chapter Twenty Seven
The Beauderriere Extended Family

Daedalus Beauderriere

Another member of the family that should have been locked up was **Daedalus Beauderriere**. He considered himself a literary critic and would send critiques of things he had only half heard about to local and national periodicals.

He was employed only once, by the Lower Undercarriage Clarion that has a circulation of under one. After leaving Clarion, Daedalus toured the world looking for even more erotic literature.

He had to give up his position lecturing on Pornographic Literature at the university when his lectures became more graphic than porno.

His test papers soon gave over to practical exams involving himself, a suitable young person and the stationery cupboard. Daedalus now spends his time in a twilight home for the bewildered with just his memories and some rather good videos. Gone are his flowing locks, he fashionable clothes and his libido. He can be seen padding around the grounds in his cardigan and slippers, nothing else, searching for his lost youth.

Unfortunately his lost youth is working in a fast food restaurant in Chigwell and declined to be interviewed. Here are a few of his insights into literature

Daedalus Beauderriere
Literature Unleashed

Understanding J.K.K Rowlkien

J K Rowlkien's Lord of the Philosopher's Ring is, on the surface, a classic fantasy tale of good over evil. Rowlkien's central character, the young Harry Baggins, is a hubble (a non-human creature) who finds himself suddenly enrolled in Rivenwarts, an ordinary school for ordinary people.

We all know how the story goes, Harry is soon in possession of the philosopher's Ring. Blah, blah. That's all very entertaining, but it's the underlying meaning of the work that has always intrigued me.

The sexual content of Rowlkien's masterpiece is thinly veiled in what one might refer to as a not very good invisibility cloak. For example, Baggins is always inserting his hairy, but deft finger into the Philosopher's Ring and on virtually every page we find him thrusting a Nymphus 2000 between his non-human thighs.

He also has a peculiar relationship with aging hippy headmaster Professor Gandledore, played by the excellent Richard E Grunt in the feature film.
Rowlkien sets out to illustrate Baggins' sexual leanings by having him come out of the closet-under-the-stairs-that-lead-to-the-shire so early in the book. The Lord of the Philosopher's Ring is a work bestrewn with phallic symbolism and erotic metaphors.

Stripped of his powers, the villain of the piece, Lord Gollumort takes up residence in the sweaty loin cloth of Bilbo Quimble, Rivenwarts' IT teacher, and it is when this is removed, (look out for one of the most erotic pieces of writing ever) that the strange scar of Harry Baggins' foreskin goes red.

Jane Eyre Unbuttoned

It is a truth universally acknowledged that Jane Eyre is probably one of the most misunderstood writers of all time. People, even those you'd think would know better, constantly muddle her up with Fanny Burney, or think, wrongly I *must* stress, that she wrote Middlemarch and was a man.

Jane Eyre is the supposedly prim little genius who wrote the famous frock frolic in which the snobby Heathcliff gets, eventually, to marry Elizabeth. But where's the sex? There's plenty of it I can assure you.

When the Vicar of Ambridge points out that Lady Catherine Deneuve of Rosings Park has several staircases he's doing it to let the reader know that Heathcliff will be hotfooting it up one of them to get to Miss Bennet's boudoir.

By that time he's already smitten with the comely country girl and has, no doubt, already dallied with her day bonnet on more than one occasion.

Remember how he said her eyes were brightened by exercise? Well how could he know? And what form of exercise does the eminent Mr Heathcliff, of Wildfell Hall, enjoy? Put it this way, he's not described as proud and upright for nothing.

Need I say more? Not really but I will. Heathcliff is clearly not the innocent we like to think him, after all, he's got a mad wife locked away in the attic. What turned her crazy I'd like to know.

And how does he pay Grace Poole? There's never any mention of her getting her wages and it's Eyre's omission of the facts that leads me to deduce that Grace was in receipt of more than a handful of thr'pennies.

An erotic book? If you take out all the 'Pray tell me's' and substitute the phrase 'afternoon tea' with a 'good hard humping' it most certainly is.

Charles Dickens - Real life? Ha!

Well, Dickens eh, Charles Bloody Dickens. What did he really know about the poor, show me a poor person who sings and dances around after a bowl of gruel. 'Consider yerself at 'ome' piss off more than likely. The poor of Victorian London were after one thing and one thing alone — GIN. Little Dorritt would prostitute herself for a pennyworth of the old Geneva. I don't think it was more gruel that little Oliver wanted more of. They were all at it in Victorian London:

The Olde Curiosity Shoppe: the Olde Ginne Shoppe probably. *The Mystery of Edwin Drood:* Ha, Edwin's Droop I should think, or more likely Brewer's Droop.

And then we have *The Pickwick Papers*. A collection of 'gentlemen' form a club. Drinking club probably. Samuel Pickwick, if that's his real name!, popping off every now and then to Dingley Dell and upsetting Kathleen Harrison. Then he promised to marry Mrs. Bordello and then wheedled out of it.

Then there's that Sam Weller, he's so pissed he can't say his V's. They are all on the piss. Charles Dickens, its all humbug!

Shakespeare What Was In His Pounce Pot?

What is it with Shakespeare, most of his works are a load of old rubbish and should be updated for the modern world:

Much Ado About Nothing should read;
Much Ado About Bollock All: Three and a half hours of theatrical bollocks put on solely for the season tickets holders to enjoy.

King Lear should read;
King Lech: Old King is bothered by his three daughters attitude to his pornographic drawing collection.

The Merchant of Venice should read;
The Merchant-Ivory of Venice: Two period costume drama a makers visit the city of canals to get a piece of the action

Romeo and Juliet should read;
Alfa-Romero and Juliet: 13 year old nymphomaniac falls in love with an Italian car.

Julius Caesar should read;

Julius Seizure: Roman General falls victim to a heart attack thereby foiling attempts to assassinate him.

Well, if he hadn't existed we would have had to invent him, wouldn't we!

Sir Arthur Conan The Barbarian

Imagine a cold winters evening, with the rain lashing the windows of 221b Baker Street. Sitting in front of a roaring fire is the renowned Consultant Detective Sherlock Holmes, opposite him sits his faithful companion and cocaine supplier, Dr. Watson. These two men have spent too long alone in each others company to be just good friends. I mean, it is well documented that Holmes had an aversion to women.

He surrounded himself with men, Watson, Lestrade and, of course, Professor Moriarty. And look at some of the titles of his 'Adventures'; 'The Man with the Twisted Lip'; 'The Noble Bachelor'; 'The Engineer's Thumb' and the 'Adventure of the Second Stain'. I rest my case.

But the worst thing of all were his adventures with what he called his 'Baker Street Irregulars'. These were young boys who would do things for him for a shilling or two.

He was always looking at things through his magnifying glass and sucking on his Meerschaum. Very strange indeed, don't you think.

Daedalus also contributed a Hollywood Interview for Clackhorne's Magazine when he was Literary Critic.

Hollywood Interviews

Each Month one of our Columnists will interview a famous Hollywood Star. This month **Daedalus Beauderriere** talks to:

1960's Starlet *Fifi LaRoche*. Her film credits include: Lust; twenty Times A Night and I'm A Nun, Help Me Get Out Of the Habit. Miss LaRoche now runs her own Casting Agency

Daedalus: Well, Fifi, it's a pleasure to meet you at last. I have all the films that you made. Mmm, you're still looking well. I wonder if you could tell our readers how you started in the business?

Fifi: You mean in the movie business? Well, it all started when I was working as a waitress in a cocktail bar, No, No, wait a minute, that's not right, that's a song isn't it? Oh, I remember, I was a hooker in Las Vegas and one of my clients turned out to be a movie producer and the rest is history.

Daedalus: So, So, umm, this, uh, movie director got you signed to one of the big studios?

Fifi: Not exactly, are you alright, you seem to be sweating a bit, anyway, he said my talent wasn't in actually acting, he said I had something more than that, something deeper. He signed me to Erotic Studios and I stared making films straight away.

Daedalus: Was it, was it, umm, rather strange, y'know, naked and doing it, doing it with all those camera people watching. Watching as your slim, lithe body twisted into all sorts of positions, glistening, swelling, opening like an oyster...I...I

It was after this that the interview was terminated due to Daedalus being knocked unconscious by one of Fifi's stilettos.

Chapter Twenty Eight
The Beauderriere Extended Family

Sir Arthur Beauderriere

One of the strangest members of the Beauderriere Family was **Sir Arthur Beauderriere**.

Sir Arthur Beauderriere first had the idea to produce a series of inventions in the 1890's when he returned from self-imposed exile on the island of Tahiti. He had gone to Tahiti a few days after his wife requested that he refrain from allsorts of sexual congress with her as she had just joined the WSTKTHWAFU (The Women's Society To Keep Those Horrible Willies Away From Us).

Like many women of her age and class, she found sexual intercourse tiring and unnecessary. Sir Arthur left the country to meditate on his future and to shag some Tahitian women.

Sir Arthur's inventions were aimed at the sexually frustrated Victorian middle-class man, although the inventions have now lost their raison d'etre some of Sir Arthur's groundbreaking ideas still resonate. Here is a selection of his advertising posters.

The original posters were falling to pieces, so the following are my careful reconstructions of those originals.

The Most Sovereign Contraption Introduced for The Comfort of Gentlemen

Sir Arthur Beauderriere's Gonad Balconette

Lubricated with premium eucalyptus paste and extracts of foreign exotica, designed by the esteemed Arthur Beauderriere for the purpose of providing dignified regional support for noblemen of considerable proportions. Only seven POUNDS, Five Shillings and Tuppence.

The lubricated balconette's superior design and tensioned cat-gut webbing grasp the Nethers for added VIGOUR and enhancement for today's wearers of fashionable restrictive breeches. Additional FISH glue coating ensures issue concealment for weeks at a tyme.
Approved by APOTHECARIES from the Illustrious Royal Institute of Knob Preservation and Spiritual Gleanings.

The Gonad Balconette for Gentlemanlike frontal elegance. HUNTING men and courtiers alike enjoy the confidence that only the Arthur Beauderriere genital accoutrements can offer.

Mr Fitzwilliam Darcy of Derbyshire says, *"It would be insupportable to stand up in any other testicular hammock. I am a proud wearer of the balconette, my gonads speak for themselves"*
....

The Most Sovereign Contraption Introduced to Alleviate the Discomfort of Piles

Sir Arthur Beauderriere's
Pile Ointment Adaptor

A Discreet and Portable Pile Ointment Adaptor that will fit comfortably into any large Portmanteau.
The Adaptor can be used Anywhere without Embarrassment*

Sturdy British Made Instrument that uses all the Latest technology that the industry can muster!
Made of Electro-Plated Nickel Silver.

This item also comes with a swivel Magnifying Mirror for even better accuracy.

*Providing you do not mind showing off your arse to all and sundry.

....

The Most Sovereign Contraption Introduced for The Comfort of Gentlemen and Their Ladies when Partaking of their Pleasures

Sir Arthur Beauderriere's
Shy Boy/Shy Girl
Mating Apparatus for the Apprehensive

A description of this device is prohibited under the newly introduced advertising law.
The 'I am not Amused' Act of 1852 introduced by Her Most Gracious Majesty Queen Victoria upon seeing The Shy Boy/Shy Girl on display at The Great Exhibition of 1851. Any information can acquired from the Inventor and will be sent to applicants in a plain brown wrapper, No one will know!

....

The Most Sovereign Contraption for the benefit of Cook

Sir Arthur Beauderriere's
Stealth Cooker
A Culinary breakthrough in Silent Cooking

Banish the sounds of cooking that come from kitchens.
Suitable for the less well-off whose kitchen is less than 100 yards from the living area
See the Stealth Cooker on display at The Great Exhibition.

Sir Arthur Beauderriere's Apothecary Range

Sir Arthur was amongst the first of his kind to operate a Mail Order Pharmacological Service. Here are some of his efficacious remedies and appliances. All were sent our in plain brown wrapping.

OXOMORON TABLETS
for people who are so stupid they can't make gravy.
SIDE EFFECTS: Thickening and browning of the urine and the tendency to use contradictory terminology.

CRAPPO-STOP
Diarrhoea Remedy
SIDE EFFECTS: May cause Diarrhoea and Thickening and Browning of the urine and the tendency to use contradictory terminology

RUPERT NANESQUE'S SUPPORT TIGHTS
SIDE EFFECTS: Irregular shaped legs, Diarrhoea and Thickening and Browning of the urine and the tendency to use contradictory terminology

STOP-U-CUM
premature ejaculation support stockings
NOTE: These stockings have never been anywhere near Rupert Nanesque's mismatched legs.
SIDE EFFECTS: Can cause premature ejaculation, Irregular shaped legs, Diarrhoea and Thickening and Browning of the urine and the tendency to use contradictory terminology

NURSE BLOOM'S GROIN STRENGTHENING ELASTIC PANTS
The above product is not recommended for anyone with a weakness in the groinal area

SIDE EFFECTS: Groin Weakness, bruising, Can cause premature ejaculation, Irregular shaped legs, Diarrhoea and Thickening and Browning of the urine and the tendency to use contradictory terminology

WAGSTAFF AND FROGJELLY
Purveyors of Soliloquy Linctuses and Balms

SIDE EFFECTS: May cause users to speak for a very long time on one subject. Groin Weakness, bruising, Can cause premature ejaculation, Irregular shaped legs, Diarrhoea and Thickening and Browning of the urine and the tendency to use contradictory terminology.

SISTER BERNADETTE MAHOGARTY'S
Celibacy Candles

SIDE EFFECTS: Hot wax can damage your thighs, do not use when ignited. Wax damaged thighs   May cause users to speak for a very long time on one subject. Groin Weakness, bruising, Can cause premature ejaculation, Irregular shaped legs, Diarrhoea and Thickening and Browning of the urine and the tendency to use contradictory terminology

HOBSON GRONKS DANDRUFF AGITATOR

The above product is not recommended for use by people with dormant dandruff

SIDE EFFECTS: Severe headaches, agitation and dandruff, Wax damaged thighs

May cause users to speak for a very long time on one subject. Groin Weakness, bruising, Can cause premature ejaculation, Irregular shaped legs, Diarrhoea and Thickening and Browning of the urine and the tendency to use contradictory terminology.

MATRON SMALL'S ROSE TINTED GLASSES

CAUTION: May impair vision, wearers may become susceptible to headaches et al.

They all cost a fortune to research and make and didn't make Sir Arthur a single penny. It is believed he sloped off back to Tahiti and sulked.

Chapter Twenty Nine
The Beauderriere Extended Family

Gordon & Millicent Beauderriere

Another scion of the family was the not-very-resourceful **Gordon Beauderriere**. He married Millicent Dalrymple just after the First World War. As the Second World War drew to a close, Gordon was happy just to plod along. Millicent, with the hope of dragging the family out of borderline poverty and helping her beloved husband, always had ideas.

"Dwarling?" said Millicent smoothing her permanent wave efficiently. "Would you be *awfully* cross if I invented something called the teenager?" Millicent's husband Gordon put down his newspaper and looked at his wife querulously.
    "Now Millie," he said with a kindly smile, "you simply must get these silly ideas out of your head. I know it sounds fun inventing things but it's hard work and you're unlikely to make any money. And anyway, there are the church flowers to think about and doesn't that Alice Blue Gown of yours need repairing?"
    "Yes I know Dwarling." said Millicent quickly making an origami model of the Titanic out of an old ration book.
"I wasn't thinking of inventing teenagers *now!*" she laughed, "I plan to wait until the 1950's, after all Susan and Robert will be grown up by then so I'll have more time."
    Gordon sighed and, polished his Bakelite meerschaum. "Come on you old silly, let's not have any more talk of inventions. You've got to think about blanching that pig's head for supper and didn't I overhear you offering to sieve old Mrs Heaton's powdered egg for her?" Millicent bowed her head.
"Yes Dwarling," she said mournfully, "but I just thought that inventing the teenager would get us out of this awful financial mess. I've thought it all through. I've got an idea for coffee bars and something I might call Rock 'n' Roll."

Gordon adjusted his monocle and stood up. His hands grasped the back of an armchair, crushing Millicent's hand-embroidered anti-maccassar. He was angry now.

"We went through all this when you had that soppy idea about telephones you carry around in your pocket. Now let's just forget all about hare-brained schemes, you sit and darn your Lyle stockings and I'll get us both and Eccles cake shall I?" Millicent smiled to herself. Gordon was a simply marvellous husband.

"Promise you're not *awfully* cross Dwarling." she pleaded.

****

"Dwarling?" said Millicent as she blacked her grate with gusto. "Would you be *awfully* cross if I invented something called the Dildo?"

Millicent's husband Gordon toyed with the buttons on his fly and looked at his wife sensuously.

"Now Millingtony-poopsylove," he said with a kindly flick of his head, "you simply must get these silly ideas out of your head. You invent something new every month and quite frankly I find it arousing. And anyway there's that plan of the Festival of Britain to look over and weren't you supposed to be entertaining Mrs Hartlepool's Polish friend this afternoon?"

"Yes I know Dwarling." said Millicent deftly producing a script for Tommy Handley's ITMA show."

"I wasn't thinking of inventing the Dildo now!" she laughed, "I plan to wait until the late 1970's, Susan and Robert will be off our hands so I'll have more time."

Gordon coughed and, buffing his Bakelite braces aggressively, said, "Come on old girl, let's not have any more talk of inventions. You've got to think about making some pigs foot jelly and didn't I overhear you offering to throw a street party for the orphans? Millicent cast her eyes downward.

"Yes Dwarling," she said sorrowfully, "but I just thought that inventing the Dildo would get us out of this hateful, hateful financial mess. I've thought it all through, simply every woman would have one either in or on their bedside table. Gordon removed his trousers and thrust his hands deeply into Millicent's cami-knickers. He was aroused now.

"We went through all this when you had the idea of camps for people to go on holiday to. Now let's just forget all about cloud cuckoo land ideas, you sit and hold my member and I'll give you such a nice surprise!"

Millicent smiled to herself. Gordon was the most divine husband in the world. "Promise you're not *awfully* cross."

****

"Dwarling?" said Millicent rinsing her Oxo tin confidently, "would you be *awfully* cross if I invented something called the Personal Computer?"

Millicent's husband Gordon toyed with the keys to his potting shed and looked at his wife nervously.

"Now Millington-poopsy," he said with a kindly nod of his head, "you simply must get these silly ideas out of your head. You invent something new every month and quite frankly I find it disturbing. And anyway there's that doodlebug to polish and weren't you supposed to be entertaining Mrs Hartlepool's American friend this afternoon?"

"Yes I know Dwarling." said Millicent deftly producing a batch of fresh Spam fritters for the W.I. fete." I wasn't thinking of inventing the personal computer now!" she laughed, "I plan to wait until the late 1980's, Susan and Robert will be of retirement age and living away from home by then so I'll have more time." Gordon sighed and, buffed his Bakelite Gramophone aggressively.

"Come on old horse, let's not have any more talk of inventions. You've got to think about making some jelly for the pigs party and didn't I overhear you offering to throw the orphans out in the street? Millicent cast her eyes downward,

"Yes Dwarling," she said sorrowfully, "but I just thought that inventing the personal computer would get us out of this dreadful financial mess. I've thought it all through, simply everyone would have one by the year 2003!"

Gordon removed his bicycle clips and thrust his hands deeply into his trouser pockets and idly fingered his dibber. He was furious now.

"We went through all this when you had that lame idea about cloning sheep. Now let's just forget all about cloud cuckoo land ideas, you sit and hold my dibber and I'll get us both a lovely cup of Horlicks shall I?"

Millicent smiled to herself. Gordon was a the most divine husband in the world. "Promise you're not *awfully* cross Dwarling." she pleaded.

****

"Dwarling?" said Millicent smoothing her floral apron happily, "would you be *awfully* cross if I invented an innovative new television programme?" Millicent's husband Gordon put his copy of Manly Things Weekly down and looked at his wife querulously.

"Now Millsy," he said with a care-worn smile, "you simply get these silly ideas out of your head. You invent something every month and quite frankly I find it unbecoming. And anyway there's the White Elephant stall to think about and weren't you supposed to be re-setting old Mrs Hartlepool's victory roll this afternoon?"

"Yes, I know Dwarling." said Millicent quickly making an exquisite ball gown out of some scraps of newspaper.

"I wasn't think of inventing the television programme *now*!" she laughed, "I plan to wait until the late 1990's, after all, Susan and Robert will be dead by then so I'll have more time."

Gordon sighed and, polishing his Bakelite brogues, said, "Come on you old ninny, let's not have any more talk about inventions. You've got to think about broiling that old show for supper and didn't I overhear you offering to help demolish the Jones's Anderson Shelter?" Millicent bowed her head.

"Yes Dwarling," she said mournfully, "but I just thought that inventing a really popular television programme would get us out of this dreadful, dreadful financial mess. I've thought it all through, the contestants on the show would be normal people who crave fame and fortune, the camera's would be on them constantly and…"

Gordon adjusted his tiepin and stood up. He grasped the tea trolley, upsetting Millicent's freshly made Parsnip Knickerbocker Glory. He was angry now.

"We went through all this when you had the lame idea of inventing a machine that washed the dishes for you. Now let's just forget all about your pie in the sky ideas, you sit and listen to the BBC Home Service and I'll get us both a glass of cordial shall I?" Millicent smiled to herself. Gordon was a completely wonderful husband, "Promise you're *awfully* cross Dwarling." She pleaded. Millicent was an enterprising woman, unfortunately her husband was a git and a Beauderriere.

Millicent also did a Hollywood Interview for Clackhorne's Magazine.

Hollywood Interviews

Each Month one of our Columnists will interview a famous Hollywood Star. This month **Gordon Beauderriere's wife Millicent** talks to:

Todd Thrust, Romantic lead of such films as: 'Now Daytripper; 'Encounter in Briefs'

Millicent:	Hello Dwarling, I hope you don't mind me asking you a few little questions.
Todd:	Of course not, ask away.
Millicent:	You acted in some memorable films with such beautiful actresses, did you ever become romantically involved with any of them?
Todd:	Of course, we were young and hot in those days! You're very beautiful. Are you married?
Millicent:	Oh yes, to a dwarling man, Gordon, we spent many an evening polishing his meerschaum.
Todd:	Sounds rather boring, have you ever considered leaving him?
Millicent:	Once or twice...but not yet.
Todd:	Come away with me, I can make you happy; this husband of yours sounds a right prick.
Millicent:	I can't, not yet, Susan and Robert, my children, still need a happy loving home, perhaps later.
Todd:	Oh well, I must be going.
Millicent:	Promise you not awfully cross!

Chapter Thirty One
The Beauderriere Extended Family

Compton Beauderriere

Another enterprising and very accommodating member of the Beauderriere family was Compton Beauderriere. He was born Constance Grace Beauderriere in 1956.
His father, a Beauderriere and his mother, a farmers daughter never married and he bore the label of bastard all his young life.

He was sometimes called a bastard by people who never knew his parents or their marital status. His deep interest in, and unrivalled grasp of, languages stemmed from living in a multi-lingual environment in no less than forty-three countries.

He is never happier than when he is being able to use his talent with his tongue in any corner of the world. He has travelled almost everywhere, from the dusty streets of the souk to the plush carpets of the Raffles Hotel in Singapore. Here are some articles he wrote.

Compton Beauderriere's
Language Workshop
"My tongue is my passport."

It happens all to often. One finds oneself nonchalantly strolling the boulevard, one's *veste de toile* draped with *faux pas* and *pif* about one's shoulders, pondering the delights of purchasing exotic pets whilst abroad.

Unfortunately, no matter how jauntily one's cap might be set, there is the constant risk of failing to flatter the rosy-cheeked *Verkäufer der Tiere* in the *magasin de bêtes*. The thrill of acquiring, for example, a newly broken in Andalusian Stallion in some godforsaken corner of the globe very often causes us to take leave of our senses. But, it is imperative, particularly when abroad, to compliment the lowly *commerci-gente*.

Here I give you astonishingly simple to learn phrase. I guarantee that, not only will you impress the humble natives but you may well find yourself flying home in your private jet, as I do, with a little bonus in your hand.

And how wonderful to know that you acquired such a gem for such a bargain price. The rules? Flatter, bargain, and fleece. *Viola*

"Excuse me, I'm interested in purchasing a boa constrictor, and may I remark upon your very progressive boils."

In French: Excusez-moi, je suis intéressé à acheter, un constricteur de boa, et peux je remarque sur vos ébullitions très progressives.

In German: Entschuldigen Sie mich, bin ich interessiert, and, eines Boa constrictor zu kaufen, und kann ich erwähne nach Ihren sehr progressiven Blutgeschwüren.

In Italian: Scusilo, sono interessato nell'acquisto del constrictor del boa e posso io rilevo sui vostri boils molto progressivi.

Panting For it

Hi, it occurred to me, as I sauntered flamboyantly through the piazza last week that communication with the humble natives, although easy for a smooth tongued *bon vivuer* like myself, can prove difficult for those whose experience of travel is limited.

For example, as I sat in the street café. The foam from my *pan chocolát* frothing delectably on my lips I noticed an English person trying to tell the lithe, olive-skinned waiter that he desired a plate of egg and chips.

Quelle disaster! The Englishman, an insult to an Italian suit if there ever was one, was getting nowhere and yet with a wink, a smile, and a quick massage of the waiter's *hurt Gefuhle*

I easily managed to procure the aforementioned platter of *eouf & frites* without so much as raising my voice. A miracle? Not at all, just a question of adopting the simpatico attitudes of the *indigenes* and learning a few simple to understand phrases.

I find it helps to carry a gentleman's handbag when abroad and, if you really want to fit in with immaculately dressed and handsome young Latinos, wear tight buff coloured trousers, remembering never put the keys to your Alfa-Romero in your pocket. It ruins the cut of the cloth and distorts the otherwise impressive *taglio del vostro fiocco*.
So remember, tight pants and a smooth tongue. *Viola!*

"Excuse me, handsome young subservient being with thighs of astonishing firmness, kindly bring me some regional delicacies and other morsels."

In French: Excusez-moi, jeune être subservient beau avec des cuisses de la fermeté étonnate, apportez-avec bonté moi quelques délicatesses régionales et d'autres morsels.

In German: Entschuldigen Sie mich stattliches junges subservient Sein mit Schenkeln de erstaunlichen Festigkeit holen Sie mir irgendeine regionale Zartheit und andere morcelgruebershcnitzel freundlich.

In Italian: Scusilo essere subservient giovane belle con le coscie fermezze astonishing gentilmente portimi alcune squisitezze regionali ed altri morcelli.

Dress to Impress

Not so long ago I happened to be strolling, a touch of lightness in my step, along the narrow cobbled streets of Naples.

"*Champignons!*" I exclaimed to myself as my chiffon waistcoat became ensnared on the horns of a passing goat.

It was then I realised, in a flash of *fleur de lis*, that chiffon is not commonly worn amongst peasants. Have they learned nothing from Gina Lollobrigida I wonder?

But I digress. Dressing appropriately when abroad is a real skill, fine if you're me, the sort of person who floats on a cushion of supreme confidence all over the world. But what about those of you, your Foreign-English dictionary clasped nervously to your chests, who simply haven't a clue?

Well, the first thing to remember is that your luggage, unless you're travelling by private jet, is likely to end up lost in Richard Branson's cargo chute or some such hell hole. So, in order to maintain your *frere jacques* you'll need to now how to purchase stylish garments whether you're in the Gobi desert or simply back-packing in Beverley Hills.

The easy to remember phrase below will set you on the right path to being clad, head to foot, in something simply gorgeous.

Warning: Try to remember that many people from other lands have never read Harpers & Queen. So, *Buona Notte Mon Petit Filou*. Until next time.

"Hello sweet, reasonably priced seamstress found in a back street. Please run me up a flattering cerise cat-suit. I dress to the left."

In French: "Bonjour l'ouvrière couturière douce et raisonnablement eue le prix indiqué a trouvé dans une rue arrière. Veuillez me courir vers le haut d'un chat-costume flatteur de cerise. Je m'habille au gauche.

In German: "Hallo fand süsse, angemessen veranschlagte Näherin in einer rückseitigen Straße. Lassen Sie mich bitte herauf eine schmeichelnde cerise Katze-Klage laufen. Ich kleide nach links."

In Italian: Ciao il seamstress dolce e ragionevolmente valutato ha trovato in una via posteriore. Faccialo funzionare prego su un gatto-vestito adulatorio del cerise. Mi vesto il a sinistra

Picture This

Last night, whilst admiring my new friend Giuiseppe's gondola, I realised, a sudden feeling of excitement circulating in my *moules marinere's*, that my passport photograph is absolute stunning, *"Caribiniere!"* I thought, "it's simply ghastly that all globetrotters (I am the exception) make do with unflattering photographic depictions of themselves. So what can be done?

Plenty, no need to get your *broderie englais* in a twist. Prior to having your passport photograph taken I advise an intensive course of sun-shower treatment followed by electrolysis to remove any unwanted male hormones (this applies to both men and women).

Then, remembering that you're going to be shot *Capodelmonte* (head and shoulders only), select something eye catching for the neck area. A fabulous piece of costume jewellery or a scarf should do the trick.

I personally like to go for the chiselled perfection look, so it's cheeks in and a full pout. *Viola!* You'll look completely Haute Cuisine and enjoy the added bonus of being able to slip into a customs officer slip through customs without making all those tiresome declarations. To recap: ponce yourself up, pout and pull.

The phrase below will come in handy for all kinds of official situations; I used it successfully when defending myself against charges of intention to commit an indecent act on sanctified ground.

"Can you not tell from this lovely snap in my passport that I am just a happy-go-lucky free spirit whose au natural tendencies are entirely innocent"

In French: "Pourvez vous ne pas dire de cette belle rupture dans mon passeport que je suis juste un heureux vais l'esprit libre chanceux dont les tendances normales d'Au sont entièrement innocentes.".

In German: " Können Sie nicht von diesem reizenden Schnäpper in meinem Paß erklären, daß ich ein glückliches gehe glücklicher freier Geist gerecht bun dessen natürliche Tendenzen des Au völlig unschudig sind"

In Italian: "Potete non dire a da questo schiocco bello nel mio passaporto che sia giusto un felice vada spirito libero fortunato di cui tendenze naturali dell' au sono intermente non colpevoli"

Getting Personal with a Dresser

Last month a gentleman wrote to me asking to become my personal dresser/companion. The application couldn't have been better timed because, *mon boeuf bourguignon*, I have recently sprained my wrist and am unable to pop my mules on unassisted.

Enter Gerald Melton, an absolute darling of a man whose recent dismissal from the funeral parlour, he had worked there as make-up artiste for many years, was a tragedy. But as one door closes another *Porte oeuvres* as they say.

Since the interview Gerald and I have been literally inseparable. He's a complete and utter dream, always ready with a smile, a helping hand and, some people think of everything, a pot of Vaseline. A must for lubricating the bits of you that travel can make weary.

So, this month's column is dedicated to Gerald without whom I would be stark naked all of the time instead of some of the time. For those of you who aren't precious enough to merit the attention of a personal dresser allow me to elucidate.

A personal dresser is responsible for ensuring that his master is constantly immaculate. Gerald, for example, never leaves the chateau without a needle and thread; several newly pressed *items de chiffon* and a Dorothy bag filled to the brim with Estee Lauder accoutrements.

We're having so much fun together Melty (my little pet name for him) and I and hope that you will join us on our travels around the globe.

Compton also worked at Clackhorne's Magazine as their Travel Guru. He also did a Hollywood Interview.

Hollywood Interviews

Each Month one of our Columnists will interview a famous Hollywood Star. This month **Compton Beauderriere** talks to:

Troy Blushe, avant-garde director of such films as I Was A Teenage Teenager; Teenage Lovers; Teenage lovers — The Early Years.

Compton: Well Troy, Quelle mange! It's really lovely to meet you.

Troy: It's great to be here, and to talk about my new…

Compton: Yes, of course, but you're early work, mostly teenagers, how was that?

Troy: Well, it was great working with young raw talent.

Compton; Mmm, all those young people in skimpy clothes, their long hair blowing in the wind..

Troy: Oh yes, the young girls were really lovely.

Compton: Oh, you had girls as well, I didn't know that.

Troy: Yes, some of them went on to become quite established stars.

Compton: Yeah, great. who was your favourite young man?

Troy: Well, I didn't really have a favourite, they were all very good.

Compton: Place de la Concorde! You had them all!!

Troy: Well, yes, I gave them all a position…

Compton: I bet…what fun, I've just got Melty, but we try all the positions too!

Troy: You seem to be putting a sexual leaning to this interview… there was nothing like that at all.

Compton: Nothing, oh well.

At this point Compton lost interest in the interview and after a while left the room.

The whereabouts of Compton Beauderriere is something of a mystery. Compton has not been seen since shortly after employing Gerald Melton as his dresser.

Gerald spends his days looking after Compton's house and waiting for his return. Gerald shows visitors around the house but seemed reluctant to show them the cellar, although someone did manage a glance though a crack in the door and all they could see was a large trunk tied up with chiffon and leaking a strange yet pleasant smelling seepage of some kind.

Chapter Thirty One
The Beauderriere Extended Family

Kev Beauderriere

Kev Beauderriere was the outcome of a quick fumble in the wood shed between Lettice, Dowager Countess of Beauderriere and a passing vagrant who asked her if she had something warm he could slip into.

When he was born, Kev was farmed out to the local washerwoman and her husband the estate carpenter. He did not know of his antecedence until he attempted a quick fumble in the wood shed with Lettice, Dowager Countess of Beauderriere as a teenager. The Countess had to tell him that she was his mother and this seemed to cool his ardour.

Educated locally and learning the carpentering and decorating trade, he shot to fame after a brief appearance on TV when he famously miscut two MDF planks and emulsioned a 17th century marble fireplace.

Kev has always been interested in art and the like, but has no experience whatsoever.

Kev hopes to win the Turner Prize one day, and let's face it, there's no reason why he shouldn't. Kev also hopes to win the Mastermind Rose Bowl too but that's unlikely as he is fundamentally thick as two miscut planks.

His show on TV brought out many gems, these are some of them.

Kev Beauderriere's
Fine Art Course

How Can You Tell What's Good?

Allo mates, If you asked me how I judge a good picture from a crap one I'd 'ave to say that I always look at it and ask meself,

"Could me mum do that?" If the answer is yes then it's crap obviously because me mum can't paint.

Now I'm not saying that everyone should use their mum as a yardstick like I do. If your mum is good at painting then it won't work. Basically think of someone you knew at school who was rubbish at art and use them instead.

Y'see I was looking at that bloke Mondrian the other night. What a load of cobblers. I didn't like it, I wouldn't give it house room and yes me mum could do it but she's got more sense than to bother. And Pickarseole, what was the blue period about? Couldn't he afford more colours? If not why not? Them match-pots are readily available at DIY stores.

It's a con, it's like me doing up someone's place all magnolia. It's boring, it's a cop out, and it's not worth the money.

What I like is a picture where you can see what it is you're looking at. I've got this one of a boy crying. It's brilliant. I've got in my lounge next to one of a sort of green Chinese woman. It looks class with the Pierrot mirror and this thing of Big Ben made of all cogs and stuff out of a watch. See, me mum couldn't do any of that.

Sculpture for Everyone

Allo, Now I don't know about you but I couldn't be bothered to carve a woman out of marble. If you want something to stand in your lounge then you can buy these moulds from craft shops. You just pour in Plaster of Paris, wait for it to dry and that's it.

You'd have to be wrong in the head to spend half your life tackling David's bollocks with a chisel. If you like something a bit more modern then you could build a wonky brick wall, shit on the top of it and glue a tin of beans to the side. Between you and me that's what I'm entering for next year's Turner Prize.

I knocked it up last week round me Nan's. She reckons the beans'll have gone off by then. That'll just add to the value in my opinion.

Right then, sculpting. Sculpting is when you make something out of something else. Like when you get a knife and carve out Kev woz 'ere in an old tree. That's the sort of idea of sculpting only it's not quite the same cos if it was sculpting what you'd do would be get a big lump of wood and carve it into a tree and *then* carve Kev woz 'ere into it.

Actually you wouldn't carve Kev woz 'ere into it if you're name was Baz or something else so try to remember that. Oh and the other thing is that if you sculpt things then you are a sculptist. A bit like if you paint things you are a paintist. No that isn't right is it? No, I always mix them up.

Anyway, people are always asking me what sort of art I have in my house. Well, most of the stuff I've got is my own work. Original Mugtons if you like. I did a picture last week with glitter glue. It's of this Spanish Lady. I done the castanets in red.

Ming or Beauderriere Can you tell the difference?

Wotcha, I started going to pottery classes so I could make something for my daughter Tracy's wedding and Tim's wedding. I thought that they wouldn't want me to spend a lot of money on something fancy. So I decided to make them a Ming vase.

As I made the vase I wondered how all them people long ago made things out of pottery when there were no night classes to go to.

When I had finished I reckon no one could've told the difference between mine and one of that bloke Ming's.

Masterpieces Compared

Wotcha

I think that what I do is Art. It's no different to Leonardo De Caprio painting his Moaning Lisa to me putting emulsion on a wall.

Anyway, this month I have decided to compare *The Vauxhall Cavalier* by Frank Halls to *The Scream* by Edward Munchkin.

I mean what's the Cavalier got to laugh about. I mean he lost the Civil War and his boss got his head cut off. And that idiot on the bridge, if he didn't like crossing bridges, why did he cross it. What does he do, run across, no he creeps across and then stands there holding his head and screaming. Get a bleeding life. Mind you, lucky Munchkin was there with his paints, eh?

Real Painting

Wotcha, y'know, when it all comes down to it, there's not much difference between me and all those old painters, Leonardo De Caprio, Vango, Munny and Manny and the like. I slap emulsion on walls and they slap paint on canvas, the only difference is that they give 'em names. I am also like that Pickarseole bloke.

Firstly I went through my own colour period, blue, sunshine yellow and green, but I must admit it was mainly magnolia. Secondly, looking at the wife, I think I married one of 'is models.

Kev also worked for Clackhorne's Magazine as did most of the Beauderrieres. He also did a Hollywood Interview for them.

Hollywood Interviews

Each Month one of our Columnists will interview a famous Hollywood Star. This month **Kev Beauderriere** talks to:

Oscar winning Set Designer Gustav Heckler, whose films include: The Minimalist; The Bare Room and The Day After The Bailiffs Came

Kev:	Well, it's smashing to meet you. Have you always been interested in design. How old were you when you realised design was for you?
Gustav:	Nein! I vas not…
Kev:	Since you were nine years old, blimey! I didn't become interested 'til my Tracy was born. "Ad to do up her nursery, realised I 'ad a flair.
Gustav:	Sheisenkopf! Vot is das! Dummkopf!
Kev:	Thanks, yeah, I'm a sorta designer meself, but I use the mediums of paint and MDF.
Gustav	Gott in Himmel!
Kev:	Nah, got in B & Q
Gustav:	Mein films we should discuss!
Kev:	Yeah, can't say I ever saw them at the pictures.
Gustav:	Vell, nein, zay were vot you call, Cult Classics, Film Noir, House Studies, umm..
Kev:	Straight to video eh, shame.
Gustav:	Do you do ceilings?

Kev: Yeah, I could sort you out an estimate.

At least Kev got something out of it.

These days, Professor Sir Kev Mugton R.A. is everywhere. After leaving his TV programme, Kev was snapped up by a TV antiques programme to act as an expert on early 20th century shit.

His incisive insight also brought him to the attention of the University of Chigwell who offered him the Chair of 20th Century Artefacts. His was knighted soon after a substantial cheque was forwarded to the right people. Despite all of these accolades, he still pines for Mastermind Rose bowl still hoping to win it one day…fat chance.

Chapter Thirty Two
The Beauderriere Extended Family

Douglas Beauderriere

Douglas Beauderriere's interest in becoming an antique dealer was inflamed by the vast amount of profit he made from selling off various priceless family heirlooms as a child.

Beauderriere, the husband of the now penniless Lady Hilary Hampton-Beauderriere, makes regular appearances on 'Crimewatch' and is most famous for his popular daytime television programme 'The Three Auctioneers'

He produced his own Art Magazine and below are a few of his articles.

Douglas Beauderriere's
Antique Dealing

When my late mother left me her vast collection of Lalique glass I decided to sell it. I didn't get on with my mother at all so the decision to sell the collection and pocket the cash was an easy one.

Since then I've made millions simply by selling the things that people who loved me have given me as gifts. I'm fortunate that I mix in the upper circles of society and therefore many of the items I am given are valuable. Members of the Royal Family have been outstandingly generous in the past, I was once given a genuine Aboruyu Rhino Horn snuff pouch, a present from the King of somewhere, which I sold for over £20,000.

If you ever come across one of these, snap it up, they are extremely rare and, these days, would fetch something in the region of £60,000. Likewise anything by Arthur Beauderriere, the 19th century inventor, some of his earlier contraptions are selling in auction for astronomical sums. And don't overlook broken Satsuma-ware, if you see a job lot of this for sale it's well worth investing. A fragmented Satsuma tea-pot, could make you a lot of money.

Oh and the biggest tip this month is to check our classifieds, we've added an Antiques and Collectables section. Worth a browse? I certainly think so.

And remember, always sell antiques for an awful lot more than you paid for them, it's not illegal, so why not? Let 'caveat emptor' be your motto.

Collector's Codpiece

When I was a young man I stumbled upon one of our servants using a rather rusty Arthur Beauderriere Brassiere Spoon. As he was a ancestor mine, I have been fascinated, not only by Arthur Beauderriere, the famous 19th Century Innovator, but by servants, rust *and* breasts.

Sir Arthur Beauderriere was responsible for such delights as the Gonad Balconette, the Clitoral Claxon and the Clockwork Flap Smoother. All items which, I am sure you agree, changed the face of history and the faces of the users. Genuine Beauderriere Innovations are, today, highly prized, highly priced and highly desirable. A little bit like myself!

I've been a collector of Beauderrieralia for many years now and my library houses many stunning examples of the rarer pieces. It is unusual to come across mint condition Beauderrieralia, there is usually some degree of restoration required, although I would urge collectors to try to maintain the objects' original finishing where possible.

For example, most Brassiere Spoons show corrosion to the brass flinks and the leather shackling found on most boudoir accoutrements will need extensive lubricating. Replacing components of Beauderriere items can be tricky. Although they were built to the highest specification the more intricate mechanisms often suffer from verdigris markings and seizure.

A light oiling will free off any stubborn thigh clamps or anal gussets. So what are Beauderriere items worth today? A bloody fortune.

Even pieces in poor condition fetch a pretty price, in fact, with the Genitalia range, a play-worn appearance and friction marks are sought after.

Douglas was imprisoned over the disputed ownership of some antiques, he said they were his because they were in his swag bag and the person that he stole them from insisted they were his. His articles still continued but from the confines of a prison.

Douglas Beauderriere's Antique Stealing

Hello lovers of fine art, as you are now well aware, I am residing at Her Majesty's Pleasure in the maximum security wing of HMP Grymthorpe situated on the wildest of moors in some place called 'The North'.

This prison has all the comforts of home, if one was used to eating shit, pissing in a bucket and showering with 25 other men. I can assure you that I have never eaten shit or pissed in a bucket.

My only contact with the antiques world is my regular copy of 'Antiques are only for Poofs', a magazine written on toilet roll with orange crayon by my cell-mate 'Thruster'. From this I have gleaned that Formica is the new oak and that he, 'Thruster' could make a better Ming vase in the pottery workshop, I think he is an aficionado of Beauderriere.

I can only look forward to my release date. Brighter things are on the horizon, I have been chosen to be Shoelace Checker next month. 'Thruster' says I should think myself lucky to have been chosen.

He said that I will be up against stiff competition to hold my position the following month. Oh well. Hey Ho for now.

Douglas Beauderriere's
Antique Stealing

I must admit it was quite a shock to find myself here in this bleak damp godforsaken place. We are woken up with the clanging of door and rattle of keys. We pick up our buckets and line up to empty them. We then go to the canteen to eat breakfast, which is the foulest tasting muck. And then we have to work for a pittance. Anyway, it's not so bad, better than the Public School I attended.

My cell-mate has taken quite a shine to me. His name is 'Thruster' which I take is a nick-name. We all have nick-names here. I think mine is Poncy Wanker, anyway that's what they all call me.

'Thruster' has told all the other prisoners that I am his friend and his alone. He tells them that I am his 'bitch'. I think we'll get along splendidly.

Well. Antiques, not much in the way of antiques in here, but here's some advice. When you get hold of some antiques from a non-reliable source, sell them on immediately or you may end up where I am. Well, it seems it's time for a shower and I have been elected soap picker-upperer. Quite an honour I believe.

Douglas Beauderriere's
Antique Stealing

Hello lovers of fine art. I really don't care anymore. I had decided to keep my head down as 'Thruster' insists and do my time.

I can only look forward to my release date. Brighter things are on the horizon, I'm sure.

When he worked for Clackhorne's Magazine, he did interview a Hollywood celebrity whilst in prison, recently, amongst the Beauderriere Papers I came across the audio tape of it, he had to do the interview over the telephone. Here is a transcript of it.

Hollywood Interviews

Each Month one of our Columnists will interview a famous Hollywood Star. This month **Douglas Beauderriere** talks by telephone to: **Tony Crappolini, star of many Gangster Films.**

This interview was transcribed from a tape recording smuggled out by Douglas.

Douglas: Hello,....Tony...hello?

Tony: Si, 'allo!

Voice on phone: *Oi Fatty Beauderriere, get off the bleedin' phone!*

Douglas: Sorry about all that, so your films are mainly about the Mafia.. why's that?

Tony: Itsa what I know innit, you have to go with what you know right?

Voice over phone: *Alright Beauderriere, times up, get you fat stupid arse back in your cell.*

Douglas: I won't be too long now. (sound of someone being hit) Ah!!

Tony: Cell!, are you in prison Mr Beauderriere, I don't like to involve myself with criminals.

Douglas:	Ha! Ha! No, no, of course not,...Thruster stop doing that!"
Tony:	What's going on, what's he doing to you. where are you?
Douglas:	Umm..I'm on..retreat, at a monastery, to..to have a rest in my monk's cell.
Voice over phone:	*Oi, twatface, in your bleedin' cell now!*
Tony:	Who was that?
Douglas:	Er, that was ..the Father Abbot.. It's time to return to our cells for meditation. I'm on my way Father!
Voice over phone:	*Don't you bleedin' father me!*

There was then the sound of someone being hit and kicked and then the line went dead.
Nothing ever was heard again!

Chapter Thirty Three
The Beauderriere Extended Family

Marjorie Beauderriere

We now more on to another Beauderriere who, like all of them, has a deep belief that she has to solve every problem that occurs in her little village of Lower Undercarriage.

Marjorie Beauderriere's career as Advisor to the World began when, as a Brownie, she started bossing people about and giving her opinions freely. Marjorie, who has never married, recently published a book, 'Country Looks for the Woolly-Haired'. She lives in with her dog Attila. Marjorie, much to her astonishment, is a gay icon.

She spends her day, knitting, making preserves and annoying the other villagers. She regularly puts her views into the local Parish Magazine. Here are some of them.

Cross-Dressing For All Occasions

Hello Dear Readers,
Last week, while adding the finishing touches to a gooseberry tart, my telephone rang. It was an old friend of mine enquiring about cross-dressing. I'm always flattered that friends think of me when faced with tricky problems like this one and I was happy to give my advice.

First though, let me touch upon the basics of cross-dressing. It is important, if you want to cross-dress successfully, ascertain just how cross you are on a scale of 1-5 before selecting garments. Mistakes are so easily made and if you are only mildly irritated it simply won't do to wear, for example, a hat that says 'I'm going to punch your bloody lights out.'

Once you know how cross you are you can begin to assemble a suitable high impact ensemble. A tip I always find useful is one given to me by Hemingfold Bilstonemuff the late Marquis of Gallsberry.

Red is an angry colour. Simple but effective. Team a red jerkin or liberty bodice with, perhaps, toning accessories like grenade holders or matching flick knives. Shoulder pads, we don't care if they are out of fashion, bedecked with military style awards for aggression and barbarism (available from most costume jewellers) will add a real feeling of fury to your outfit.

Finally, never feel ashamed of feeling cross, it takes all sorts to make a world.

How Cross Are You Exactly?

1. Mildly put out
2. Getting a bit het up
3. Quite unreasonably furious
4. Insanely enraged/violent
5. Displaying psychopathic symptoms

Cottaging in the Village

Hello Dear Readers

I was looking through my copy of *People's Friend* the other day, when I heard a knock on the door. I opened it to find my next door neighbour Major Brashe. He was in a very agitated state. He said that he had received a summons from the courts to face a charge of cottaging.

I sat him down and poured him a generous glass of Wincarnis and tried to give him some sage advice.

I told him that there was nothing wrong with living in a cottage, I myself had been cottaging for many years and have never been summoned before the courts. The Major looked at me strangely and asked me if I had something stronger to drink, I went to my secret cupboard and opened a vintage bottle of Sanatogen Tonic Wine and offered him a glass. He downed it in one and asked for another.

I said that I hoped he hadn't had any alterations down to his cottage without referring them to the parish council because they can get quite obdurate. He mentioned he was being summoned for loitering around the public toilets in the village. I told him that the government gives grants to put conveniences in Grade 1 Listed buildings, so he would have no need to use the public ones.

I told him I had seen him near the public toilets in the company of the vicar, perhaps he could give him a hand. The major laughed and left.

Rubber for All

Hello Dear Readers,
Last week I read in my local paper that our vicar is a rubber fetishist. Needless to say there are some members of the parish who are shocked by the news. Aren't we English a stuffy lot! It's alright for us to be fetishists but not the vicar.

I was so outraged by some people's narrow views that I staged a revolt on the village green. I myself am a rubber fetishist. it think it's simply marvellous stuff, I get through, on average, nearly two pairs of marigolds per day, more if I'm gardening or going to have anything to do with the boy scouts.

And as for always having a rubber on the end of my HB, well I'm never without one. It's so easy, when jotting down a recipe for a friend, to make a mistake. Swiftly on to Wellingtons then. here in the countryside a decent pair of hard-wearing Wellingtons is a must.

I favour the green Stanley Eversfield boot with fleecy lining, they are a little more expensive but so durable and impervious to most wet substances that extra expense is well spent.

A rubber sheet when picnicking always comes in handy. Eleanor Lavishe (A Room With A View) never went anywhere without her Mackintosh Squares. I suppose that makes her a rubber fetishist too. Poo bah to this silly tendency to sneer at users of rubber.

When will we realise that we are all users? The tyres on your motor vehicle are made from rubber but you wouldn't expect to be banned from buying a ticket to the Gang Show because of it would you? I always say it takes all kinds of people to make the bright and beautiful world we live in.

Taking Drugs

Hello Dear Readers,

Every Wednesday a Drug Advice Group meets in my local Village Hall. I'm astonished by this I must say because most drugs these days come with detailed instructions as to how they should be used.

For example, the leaflet included with my migraine tablets is self explanatory. Take two pink ones at the onset of an attack and a yellow one in the midst of an attack and unload the Purdey Shotgun, it couldn't be simpler. So why the need for a Drug Advice group in our sleepy village? I went along to find out.

I was astounded to see so many unhealthy people there. It really brought the message home I can tell you. None of the attendants looked as if they could even manage to get the lid off of a bottle of aspirin let alone read the instructions. I immediately changed my tune and decided that the Drug Advice Group was a good thing.

As I was there I took the time to talk to many of the people and can safely say they went away looking absolutely amazed. It seems that they were so stunned by what I had to tell them that they no longer feel the need to attend the group. One of them said to me, "It's a waste of bleeding time coming here."

Isn't that marvellous? I was so happy to be able to help with what is such an easy to solve problem. If you think you have a problem with drugs take the time to read the leaflet and everything will turn out fine. Finally, it's nothing to be ashamed of, lots of lovely people have difficulty following instructions.

Advice about Speed

I learned at the Drug Advice Group that many young people enjoy speed. I don't understand why doing things fast was being talked about at such a group but my advice is that if you like freewheeling on your bicycle or sprinting that's your choice and it's nothing to worry about at all.

There is Nothing Wrong in Being Gay

Hello Dear Readers,
I overheard some elderly ladies at the fete last week condemning the Vicar for being gay!, I ask you, what could possibly be wrong with that. I interrupted and admonished them. I told them, that with so much misery in the world, it's nice when people openly admit they are gay. I am always gay, I enjoy a good laugh, and have many a merry thought.
    The ladies said that they shouldn't be allowed to marry each other. Preposterous! If like-minded people married each other there would be less arguments. The ladies, eyeing me strangely, said there was also the rumour that there was at least one Lesbian in the village.
    I said that, although I have never been to Lesbia, I am sure they are very nice people. And as a gay icon, people look up to me to promote merriment, laughter and gaiety. Shout it out loud, I'm Gay and proud of it!!

Marjorie, an avid reader of romantic fiction wrote three novels of her own. They were so clichéd and similar to other writers that to put them down here and let you see a truncated version of them. They are so like other writers that she used nom-de plumes not dissimilar to the originals.

Perhaps the following is the future of writing dross. I let you decide. I have called them ....

The End, the end of a clichéd story for those who can't be bothered to read a whole one.

Mind the Antlers
By Bullbar Smith

The Story so far: *Peter Masterton (a bloke with chiselled jaw and a determined, but cruel mouth) returns from safari to find that the central female character, Philippa (a young woman who has always been thought plain because she wears glasses) has had laser eye surgery and no longer dons specs.*

There is much reference to loin stirring and similar type awakenings. The ex-spectacle wearer is, obviously, now seen as highly desirable. Unfortunately, Masterton has his work cut out for him, having been dismissive and offhand with the girl throughout the entire story so far.

There is also the question of a love rival Cecil Meeks, a quiet librarian with a concave chest who has always been inordinately kind to Philippa. Will Masterton win the girl?

Of course he bleeding will because now that her vision has improved she can see that the weedy Cecil isn't shag-worthy and that hunky Masterton is. The moral to the story? Well quite clearly there isn't one. Read on!.....

Peter Masterton could feel the sweat gathering in the folds of his designer safari suit. He tossed his newly acquired set of gazelle antlers onto the four-poster bed. They meant nothing to him now. And yet just days ago, when he had wrenched them from the animal's skull he had felt his manly pride swelling.

Now though, all that seemed highly unsatisfactory. Masterton faced a new challenge. Philippa. Now that she was no longer visually impaired she could appreciate his merits and he, funny how the removal of her glasses had made him realise that she had pert full breasts, could appreciate hers.

Masterton stared at himself in the mirror and flexed his muscles.

"Not bad for an incredibly good-looking guy who's always been popular, good at sports and has loads of money." he said, running a firm hand through his glossy but unruly hair.

When Masterton heard the tentative knock at the door he knew, with the sort of absolute confidence only people in books seem capable of, that bit was her. She would have to take him as he was, safari worn and blood smeared and yet still more outstandingly desirable as anyone had the right to be.

"Come." he said, his voice rasping erotically.

Within moments he had enswathed his muscular arms around her fragile but willing body Through the flimsy fabric of her Laura Ashley blouse he could feel that she had longed for him for at least two years and had been in a state of constant and intense arousal.

"Take me Peter Masterton." she urged softly. And lying back onto the four-poster that had seen so much action in the past she toyed teasingly with her leg 'o' mutton sleeves.

"Mind the antlers." Said Peter brusquely as he entered her. The End.

Buoyed up by this first story, she attempted another. This next attempt of Marjorie's was...

Frigid Jones' Diary
By Helen Fieldmouse

The Story so far: *Frigid Jones, a dairy worker who hasn't got a boyfriend, decides to document the plight of her sex in diary format. Jones, who believes she is overweight (but-clearly-isn't-really-given-that-she-will-be-portrayed-by-someone-quite-slim-in-the-feature-film-if-one-is-ever-made) has just been ditched by neighbouring* *butcher-cum-stud Daniel Meatcleaver because his sexual needs outweighed her own.*

Frigid is just beginning to realise that apparently boring Mark D'Arsehole, a lifelong acquaintance, is a more than nice man who she has been being rude to throughout the book. Will Frigid finally peel off her great big milkmaid's bloomers and jump into D'Arsehole's paddling pool?....Read on!

Monday:
Saw Mark D'Arsehole at the Annual Churning Fete. Have not forgiven him for beating up Daniel Meatcleaver in the Pig's Trotter the other night. Wanker. Am immensely fat and incapable of getting boyfriend

Cigarettes: 0 – don't smoke am clean living country lass.

Alcohol: 0 – don't drink unless you count sherry at Christmas which disagreed with me and as probably responsible for Uncle T having his way with me under the mistletoe.

Butter: 24 tons – hand churned and dispatched to Anchor headquarters this morning.

Tuesday:
Saw Mark D'Arsehole at Agricultural fair. Felt left out. Only singleton there. Everyone else was clever and accompanied by a prize pig or some such companion. Marl v kind. Offered to drive me home in Landrover. Probably wanted sex.

Wednesday:
Mark D'Arsehole did want sex. Said no. Am still friend Wazza say am mad as Mark D'Arsehole is image of famous actor called Colin, who apparently, is highly desirable. Wouldn't know or care, haven't got a telly. Keep trying to remind people frigid.

Thursday:

Just been reminded that once frolicked naked in Mark D'Arsehole's paddling pool. Can't believe it. Am probably sex maniac who enjoys shagging to having a proper boyfriend.

Friday:
Dressed up as a dominatrix for local garden party. Chased Mark D'Arsehole through village, finally catching up with him outside the church. Got married. Ahh. Am really marvellous girl who everyone thought was pretending to be frigid and lacking in confidence...The End.

Marjorie's final attempt was...

A Cardigan Each
By Rosalind Pilchard

The Story so far: *Norma, a floral clad woman of retirement age has moved to a quaint village to pursue a peaceful lifestyle. When she has lived in the village for over six years she becomes part of the furniture and, despite the inconvenience caused by the locals constantly mistaking her for a wing-back chair, falls in love with Rodney.*

Rodney is a professional suede elbow patch restorer and part time twitcher (person of ornithological bent) who has lived with his mother all his life.

When he first meets Norma he is taken aback by her unconventionality; she wears open-toed sandals and has been abroad twice. Despite the social and mental chasm that divides them, Rodney and Norma embark upon a completely boring relationship and announce their engagement in the local paper...Read on!

"Only another four weeks Rodney, and we shall be man and wife" piped Norma.

She looked across the restaurant table at her soon-to-be-husband. Norma was happy and was eager to do all the little things that wives do for their husbands.

"I hope everything is ready for the big day, Norma." said Rodney in his nasally twang that first drew Norman to his side. Norma nodded.

"Mmm," said Norma her mouth full of broccoli. She swallowed hard.

"Everything's arranged, church, vicar, cars, I don't think we've missed anything!"

Rodney and Norma walked through the village hand in hand.

"We're very lucky to live in this wonderful place, aren't we darling?" said Norma. Rodney squeezed her hand.

"Yes, beloved, there's so much of nature around us, the flora and the fauna. And we've got such a lovely cottage to live in, nice garden, what more can we want."

They walked to the little stone bridge over the river and looked at the water.

"I'll tell you what I haven't seen much of lately," said Rodney.

"What's that my love!" purred Norma.

"Tits, Great Tits, Little Tits. he said. I've seen plenty of woodcocks, thrushes, and lots of other birds, but I'd really like to get to grips with a pair of tits."

Norma fingered her blouse buttons for a moment then thought better of it. As they walked on Rodney stopped suddenly.

"Oh No! There is something I've forgotten, I've forgotten the bridesmaids!"

They both thought for a moment, then Norma looked up and smiled at Rodney.

"Don't worry, I know exactly what they would like, we'll get them a cardigan each!" Rodney smiled. "Lovely idea!"

The End

Marjorie also did a Hollywood Interview for Clackhorne's Magazine when he was an Agony Aunt.

Hollywood Interviews

Each Month one of our Columnists will interview a famous Hollywood Star. This month **Marjorie Beauderriere** talks to:

Georgiana Dyke, star of many Lesbian Erotic Films such as 'Strummin'; 'Strappadictomy' and 'A Finger of Fudge'

Marjorie: I must say that it's a pleasure to meet you.

Georgiana: I've looked forward to this interview, I've heard so much about you.

Marjorie: Now my dear, you've made many films and there all about Lesbians, don't you think that you've been stuck in the groove?

Georgiana: Yes, all my films involved Lesbians, it's my speciality, my forte, my weakness. I am , in fact, a Lesbian. Does that surprise you?

Marjorie: Oh, no, my dear, we all have to come from somewhere. I was born in Norfolk, you were born in Lesbia.

Georgiana: Sorry, what do you mean?

Marjori The place you were born, Lesbia, you said you were a Lesbian.

Georgiana: It's not a place Marj, it's a state of mind. It's a melding, sweetie, of

	like-minded people, people of the female sex.
Marjorie:	A sort of club, a club for ladies only Like the W.I. Eh?
Georgiana:	That's right, no men allowed.
Marjorie:	What sorts of things go on at your club?
Georgiana:	Allsorts. The main occupation is to help each reach their….
Marjorie:	Potential?
Georgiana:	That's one way of putting it. But the main event is deep and dirty sex, writhing sweaty bodies, entwined in ecstasy, each achieving a marvellous orgasm.
Marjorie:	I see.. So it's really, it's just like my old boarding school, but without the lessons! What, what night of the week is it...

Chapter Thirty Four
The Beauderriere Extended Family

Peregrine Hilary Beauderriere
(Professional name: Rick Faberge)

Peregrine, or Rick as he prefers to be called, for some strange reason, is the youngest grandson of Lord Beauderriere. He shot to fame as lead singer of the 70's rock band *'Hot Knob Fellatio Megastar'*. He owns a castle in Scotland and collects expensive things.

He has been married nine times to six different blondes. Rick enjoys spending money and having sex. Sometimes the two enjoyments have had to be combined.

Now a recluse, he was tracked down by the famed Clackhorne's Magazine in the middle of the 80's and the piece below is the only surviving interview he ever gave.

Interview conducted by Ingrid Boobssen

Ingrid: *Tell us a little about yourself Pereg...Rick.*

Rick: Back in the 70's when I was a pop legend I made millions, when I finally hung up my guitar and went into property I was already a multi-billionaire with homes in all six corners of the globe.

Well a guy's gotta have somewhere to park the yacht! Resentful people often say to me, you had it easy Rick. Well sorreeey. I've been sensible enough to invest my money so why should I feel guilty?

Rich people like myself have what we, in business circles, call acumen. We invest our cash instead of spending it down the bingo. We think ahead, we buy vintage cars instead of old bangers. We take advantage of house repossessions whereas poor people generally slip up by forgetting to pay their mortgages and getting their houses repossessed.

Rich people get banks to lend them money. Poor people don't. Rich people can afford to buy whatever they want, poor people can't.

Rich men, even ugly ones, get to go to bed with attractive young women whereas poor men don't. So, how can a poor person become rich? It's easy. I did it, The Queen, God love her, has managed it and countless other people who are lucky enough to live in a capitalist society have done it too.

If you'd like to be rich but haven't a clue how to go about it, the tips in fact sheet might help. Send me the deeds of your house and a SAE and I'll help you become as rich as me.

Ingrid: *In spite of all the drugs, drink and sexually transmitted diseases, you seem to have got your head together Rick!*

Rick: As I've always had my head screwed on straight I find it hard to believe that people actually go mad. I mean, what is the point of it? Given the choice I know I'd rather be the together kind of guy I am than the sort of dribbling imbecile I might be if I chose to go nuts. I guess I'm just lucky that I'm perfect.

But what about those who aren't? Well sod them. To be honest I haven't time for people who go loopy. If they want to waste their lives having nervous breakdowns and hearing voices that's their business. There's also the question of clothes. How many mad people have you met that are natty dressers? None. That's another thing that puts me off the whole cranky route.

I wouldn't take kindly to having to wear trousers that are too short for me or don my Pierre Cardin shirts inside out. Mad people, on the other hand, love all that and they do it for attention. Same with talking to themselves.

Can't they get mobiles for Christ's sake? That way at least they'd blend in with all the superior people like myself who are never off their phones.

Ingrid: I see from these items around your house that you consider yourself quite the collector.

Rick: Being a multi-billionaire means that my homes are strewn with tasteful objects. I guess I'm lucky to have an eye for what works and what doesn't. But it isn't just about money. It's about style.

I was trying to explain the difference between tasteful and tacky to my girlfriend, Anouskana, the other day but there wasn't much point. She's had a little too much bubbly the night before and wasn't listening. But for the benefit of those of you who haven't been drinking Timotei I will explain.

There a difference if you can't tell then you're probably the tacky sort. Test yourself. Have all the women you know got fingernails with very white square ends? If yes, then you've got taste. You can spot tasteful people in many ways, their all year round tans are a big clue for starters. And the addition of leopard-skin to the bedroom is a subtle indicator of a stylish and tasteful person.

Tacky people simply turn their noses up at some of the black ash effect furniture on the market these days preferring dusty old stuff that should have been chucked out years ago. In my Spanish villa I've gone for the minimalist look. Just one padded vinyl mini bar and water bed per room. No need to over do it. That would be tacky.

Likewise to many gilded gargoyles, I just have the one musical Elvis water-feature and statuette in the hallway which adds impact.

Ingrid: Are you still in contact with family and friends?

Rick: Well, it's obvious really, the best people to have around you are friends. I mean your family know all your little secrets and such like, whereas you can still impress your friends with your money, flash cars and big houses.

I haven't seen any of my family since I told them all to piss off and leave me alone. They were just scrounging windbags, always moaning about how granny needs a new hip, cousin Charlie hasn't worked for years and just needs a little bit of cash to get him started self-employed and how they haven't been able to find a donor for my dad.

What the hell does he want a kebab for, his heart is weak, and a greasy one would kill him. No, it's best to stick with your friends, you know they only want you for your money, they don't try the *'we're family Ricky'* rubbish on you. Stick with your friends, at least you know where you stand. As Ingrid left, Rick called out to her and left here reeling with a pithy and true (his words) piece of observation.

If Peter Cook, Robin Cook and Captain Cook opened a bistro and helped in the kitchens does it necessarily follow that the broth would be unpalatable?

Rick also did a Hollywood Interview for Clackhorne's Magazine.

Hollywood Interviews

Each Month one of our Columnists will interview a famous Hollywood Star. This month **Rick Faberge** talks to:

Multi-millionaire Film Producer Stanley Eversfield.

Rick: So you're rich are you..how rich?

Stanley: It's rather passé talking about money, don't you think?

Rick:	No, not if you've got stacks of it. I'm stinking rich, mega-rich. I am incredibly wealthy.
Stanley:	I've had a riding boot named after me!
Rick:	Oh yeah, I've got lots of illegitimate kids named after me, beat that!
Stanley:	My name will go down in the history of film making!
Rick:	I was a famous rock star!
Stanley:	I've never heard of you!
Rick:	I've never seen any of your films!
Stanley:	I don't want you to!
Rick:	Well, I'm not!
Stanley:	I've never heard any of your songs!
Rick:	Oh, bollocks!

We will leave them comparing the size of their willies.

Chapter Thirty Five
The Beauderriere Extended Family

Lord Beauderriere

The Beauderriere/Verruca Scandal

Perhaps the most explosive documents found were those concerning Lord Beauderriere and the Countess de Verruca, both of these names mean nothing now, but in the 1920's, they were part of a scandal that shook the world.

I think that before we start on this part of the story, I should tell you a little of the history of both the Beauderriere family and Verruca's. I will start with the Beauderriere lineage, as it is the most ancient.

The line of the Lord Beauderriere stretches back in to the mists of time. Many of them have been mentioned earlier. The late Lord Beauderriere was descended from the lineage of Charlemagne lesser-known brother, Engelbert the Wary. This forebear did nothing to even make a dent in history, but as he was the brother of the Holy Roman Emperor, he had to be put to some use and that must be as far away as possible.

Well, as history doesn't report, Engelbert was given the province of Puritania to govern. And as not mention of this place was never mentioned in history, we can assume that nothing exciting ever happened. The late Lord's family came to England with Emperor Napoleon III and the Empress Eugenie and eventually settled in property owned by the family in Oxfordshire.

As far as the Countess's title, it seems that this title goes back to 1793 in Sardinia when one Antonio Marlarki, assisted in repelling an invasion by the French. His brave action caused him to be honoured with the title Count de Verucca, the name coming after the little fishing village he lived in. With the title, his sardine business prospered and was graciously given the hand of Princess Violette de Naples, daughter of the King of Naples.

The Verucca line prospered and Gabriel Marlarki, the 6th Count de Verucca married the subject of this and subsequent chapters.

The late Lord Beauderriere, at that time, was Ambassador to the Republic of Calimari. He had left their homeland, deep in the forests of Britain to come to this tiny island lost in Mediterranean Sea. The island of Calimari had no industry or indigenous skills, what it did have was tons and tons of birdshit, called guano in polite circles.

It exported this avian excrement all over the world where it was used as fertiliser. With the income from this Calimari was able to import fine wines, cars and penniless aristocrats to give this gallstone of the Med some kind of veneer.

Apparently, it was on the island that Lord Beauderriere first set eyes on the Countess. She was standing on the runway watching the skies. He turned to his aide-de-camp and asked whom she was. "Bugger knows" replied his aide, Arnold Steppinton, "perhaps some old drunk". His Lordship nodded in agreement and they walked to the car and were driven to the embassy to take up residence. She was, he was informed later, The Countess de Verruca, a wealthy widow who lived on the island in a château in the hills.

He next saw the Countess at the Ambassadors Reception, she was dressed, which I believe was quite unusual for her! She arrived with, spent most of the evening deep in conversation with, and left with, the local Police Chief. It was only later that his Lordship found out that they had been handcuffed together. Apparently, she had been arrested earlier in the day for smuggling some dope into the country.

The dope in question was the Honourable Timothy Short-Cummins, a distant cousin of Beauderriere's. The Countess has always been something of an enigma. Where she came from nobody know or even cares. She sails through life like a galleon in full sail and has the stopping power of a gigantic oil tanker at full speed.

His Lordship had decided to write a biography of the Countess, in his retirement years and had decided not to soften any blows in the exposé of the Countess. He decided to tell all, anything he was not sure of, he would fabricate. It would be a story of sex, alcohol, roistering and many deviant animal acts. He would tell everything about the Countess's early years, when as a dancer of little skill, she toured the whole of Europe, playing to anyone who would give her the price of a drink.

Whomever she met, she would drag down to her depths and many a young aristocrat has lost his family's fortune and his trousers keeping her in the style to which she had become accustomed. As soon as it was known that he was going to write this tome, He received letters of support as well as letters of condemnation.

It became the most talked about event of the century. Ever since he muted that he might write a book on the Countess, claim and counter claim were publicly hurled at him regarding the honesty and veracity of the contents and of the subject of the book. Lawyers and friends, friends who are lawyers and friends who know lawyers have all put their thoughts down on paper to vindicate or entrap the Countess or myself.

Within these pages, you will find the warts and all story and a record of the most dramatic libel and defamation trial since that of Oscar Wilde.

The whole thing started after he had sent the first draft of his book to his Literary Agent Hiram Gitt for is comments:

The Uncensored Verruca
The Life of Countess Guilietta de Verucca
By Lord Beauderriere

I have been asked by my publishers to write a brief history of that infamous one-time courtesan and full-time imbiber, The Countess de Verucca. As I sit in my favourite wicker chair with my bare buttocks lending themselves to the chair's intricate yet not unbecoming designs, my mind goes back the those halcyon days on the island of Calimari, when as a young man, I first met the Countess.

I was Ambassador to the island. I had left my homeland to come to this tiny island lost in Mediterranean Sea.
It was on the island that I first set my eyes on the Countess. She was standing on the runway watching the skies…

His Lordship was rather pleased with the manuscript; he had always thought that he had a literary bent. With great reverence he placed the sheets of handwritten paper into an envelope, borrowed a stamp from his butler and sent it off.

His Literary Agent, Hiram Gitt, wrote back to him after receiving the manuscript. He did not think that that git, Gitt would act as he did.

HIRAM G GITT
Literary Agent to the Nobility

Dear Lord B, Thank you for the initial draft of your book 'The Uncensored Verucca' will peruse and get back to you. My first impression is that it is going to shock many people and cause quite a controversy. I have sent a letter of thanks to the Countess, how did you get her to agree? Hiram

This stupid act by a stupid man resulted his Lordship receiving rather a curt letter from the Countess's solicitors, which did nothing to help his Lordship's temper. Lord Beauderriere was not a man to suffer fools or anyone gladly.

He had an innate distrust and dislike for lawyers ever since he lost what was to be called *The Leather Trials of Milton Keynes*, but that is another story The letter had all the vitriol concomitant with legal missives. It is quite easy to visualize the lawyer, sitting in his office, rubbing his hands at the chance to bring a good man down. I do consider myself a 'good man'.

His Lordship was very philanthropic in his younger days. He followed the example of that great Victorian, Gladstone, and visited the rather seedier areas of London, bestowing largesse on the poor unfortunates that plied their trade on the streets. Those poor girls, all they had to look forward to was a life of degradation and abuse.

As he drove his Bentley slowly along the kerb, many of them would offer their services to him. Not wanting to disappoint them, he took pity and allowed them the use of his car and body.

However, I digress, he received the letter from the Countess's solicitors and it threw him into a rage. The Countess's solicitors, Hanns, Neece & Boompadasey wrote:

Hanns, Neece & Boompadasey
10 Extortion House Legal Lane London W1

Dear Lord Beauderriere (hereafter referred to as 'that bastard')
I am instructed by my client, (hereafter referred to as 'my client') the Countess de Verucca, to give you formal notification that the publication of your forthcoming biography 'The Uncensored Verucca', (hereafter called 'that crap book') will not be welcomed by my client and that my client hereby denies that there is any truth in any of the content contained therein.

I will henceforth, on the instruction of my client, issue forthwith a legal document thereby outlining he legalities of this matter and hereby propose to commence immediate legal action against you which, in the light of the situation, will be delayed for a period not exceeding fourteen days and no less that then four days.

Provided that the above specifications are adhered to in full, without exception and in a manner thereby outlined in the lay-by. Not withstanding full responsibility for the outcome of any omissions you may have deliberately made to favour the logistical impact, either probable or calculated in the light of unmeritorious solicitations, I think.

In closing, I should further suggest that our client, the prestigious and virtually flawless Countess, has been the subject of this kind of literary calumny before. The fact that the books have never been published and that the authors are living out a squalid existence in the most unsavoury part of Milton Keynes leads me to surmise that a letter of total retraction is heading out this way from your office.

In closing, I should like to suggest that the overall concept of your book, i.e. that the Countess is a 'flatulent, alcoholic, narcissistic old tart and let us prove it in print' is particularly alarming, considering its accuracy. Such accuracy achieves nothing, particularly in a court of law. In closing, we say 'ready for the scrum down'.

Please feel free to enter into written exchanges with us, we charge the Countess an exorbitant fee for these letters.

Yours truly,
Jeremiah Hanns

It was not really the content of the letter that annoyed him; it was the implication that he did not know her history. What followed then was an unsolicited letter to his Lordship from the lady herself. It's composition reflected her life of booze, blokes and bad schooling. It read:

Countess Guilietta de Verucca
La Spinetta Santa Maria Boulevard Monaco

Jou Count

I am learned today of jour intentione to publicato a libre about my life, thees is the cause of great distress to me because I am not even knowing jou.

Ow cen jou write la historic of me when it id only one time that we rubbed soldiers together? Thees occasion I recall well, I was avisiting England alone, I ad ben saffering such pains in my foots and looked to your beluvved country for piss and tranquillizers. Jou were introduced to me by our mutant friend Lord Livid. Jou signore, were a Biological Professore at the time easily can bring to my minds ears the way jou would twist jour moustache at my entrance.

Now I am knowing jou have became the Count of Lovelyarse and life is avery different for jou. But I think still jou are the same person who always spoke of the leatherworks wiz such excitement. Yes, I am forgetting this side to jour caricature. Even now I am regretting letting jou near my thighs with the garlic butter, but zat is anuzzer tale.

As jou are knowing, I was a vagina and very innocent. Although our meeting was in briefs, I sink I am good enuff judge of caricature to know jou are a feelthy purveyor interested in only one things.

I am thinking now that jou compost this biographia in an effort to revenge me for refusing jour sexual advancements at me all those yearse ago.

Signore Prettybum, no one will see the truth in jour book. Only it can be tail of the fairies for it is a work of friction. I have spoken very wildly with my solicitors who are determined to go done on jou and read eagerly what jou get out.

The firm is Hanns, Neece & Boompadasey who are very good at legal fuck ups. Jou must ave jour back watched jou big count, and know always this, I have lots of frens in lots of places, very high up and very low down. I also ave sum frens in the middle, but I don't talk about them. I ope jou are getting the illustration that I ave some angry against jou.

I also wish for jou to do some reading between the tracks and see that maybe I ave the sad feeling between my bosoms. Hif only we could still be good frens now they say I am no longer a vagina. I have lost my sweet girly insolence and would now be interested in the working of the leather.

The life for me is lonely since my dear usband choked to death while masturbating on some chickens when we last dined in Rome. Some of the nights when I ave drunk a leetle too much wine, I sink to myself that perhaps I now could enjoy the study of biology.

Alas signore, you are determined to expose my private parts to zee world. I ave nothing more to say on this matter, I am sinking only that thins could ave been very different if jou ad not taken jour nib in jour hand and do this painful and intrusive probing of me.

Guilietta de Verucca

There then followed a series of letters supporting one or other of the parties.

**Uccello's
Ristorante Classico**
23 Via della Bovine **Roma Italia**

My dear Lord Beauderriere

One of my customers is tell me that you wish to make book of la Bella Contessa de Verruca. I am a good friend of her and of Vincenzo, her late husbands who died here in my own beautiful restaurant.

I have remembered this evening so clearly, La Contessa was 'ow you say? Arse ratted. She have a lot of thirst that night. She drink some lot of vino and talk all the time about Biology. She go crazy about the new leather chairs I have put in my restaurant. She embarrassed the waiter Paulo, she keep pulling on his moustache. Her husband is get green with envious and him say to her "I am want to kill you now, you old slipper!"

La Contessa she just laugh, she slap the face of the husband and eat her spaghetti. Vincenzo, he try not to notice her and enjoy his chickens. Next he is making a lot of noise that disturb my other customers, he is gone blue and have fall over and make a lot of damage and fiasco.

La Contessa she go white with shock, she take of the jacket of Vincenzo and go through the pockets, next she try to do the kisses of life. I say leave me alone Contessa, take your tongue out of my mouth, and look after your husbands. It is too late; I telephoned the paparazzi and the Vatican. We did everything that we could to save the Count and all of us felt sad because he had not paid his bill.

I have let the Contessa have the meal free of the charge because I feel sorry for her. I have not seen her since that night and she stills owes for a bottle of Chianti she drunk.

I have in my possession the last words of Count Vincenzo de Verruca. He write them down on a napkin because he had no speech because of the chickens choking him. I am like to show you the contents of the napkin, but I would want a lot of money first.

I often sit in my restaurant in the early hours of the morning when it is quiet and remember the Count writing on the napkin and it seems to me perhaps he could have written a cheque as well. I looks forward to you contacting me.

Yours Guiseppe Uccello

He received letters from all and sundry!

The McNutters Psychiatric Institute
Knutt Lane Chelmsford

Dear Lord
In my vork as a psychiatrist, I am often asked ze following difficult qvestion, 'Am I mad Doctor?' Usually in answer to zis I am happy to be able to say, jah, mein patient, you are stark staring bonkers. Simple and straight to ze point und no

messing. However, life vould be very boring if ve vere all sane, or loopy to ze same degree.

Sometimes I have come across patients whose diagnosis completely eludes me. Although zis is a little tiresome, it is at ze same time challenging. Ze most fascinating and absorbing case I ever had to vork on vas zat of a jung soldier who had suddenly slipped into a severe state of Traumatic Shock Ejaculation.

His continual erections had ze effect of depriving his brain of blood supply and hence oxygen until he vas little more than a blithering imbecile incapable of speech. It vas not long before he lost all logical thought patterns. When I came across him at a railway station in Berlin. I assumed that ze man vas a 'mental' casualty of war, disturbed by ze horrific sights he had vitnessed during active service. But my prognosis Vas wrong. I only realised ze gruesome nature of ze cause of zis mans psychosis when, after seven months of futile and ineffectual therapy, he vas visited by ze Countess de Verucca.

My patient reacted so severely on seeing her that I had to attempt to physically remove her from ze room. She was not willing to depart and clutched at my lederhosen with I caused a diversion so that he could escape by taking her there and then on the commode. I hope that this information is useful to you.
Yours Dr. Freidrich von McNutter

Ye Olde Fetishists
Leatherworks & Saddlery
The Old Forge, Upper Mares Bottom Buckinghamshire

Mr Hanns
Hanns, Neece & Boompadasey

Dear Mr Hanns

I was deeply alarmed to hear that the Lord Beauderriere was in some kind of trouble following his recent declaration that he is to publish a written work on the life of the Countess de Verucca. I am a humble belt maker and worked my way to the top of my profession and I am now proud to be Managing Director of this establishment.

Many years ago when I was just a hands-on man on the factory floor, I had the privilege of becoming acquainted with his Lordship, who was at this time teaching biology at a ladies seminary. Whilst lubricating a rather exquisite piece of hide, I slipped into something of a reverie, my thoughts were miles away as I gently rubbed liberal quantities of eel mucus into the divinely leathery skin.

It was some moments later when I realised that his Lordship was on his knees in front of me salivating profusely. From that day on Lord Beauderriere and I have enjoyed a particularly piquant friendship, a friendship that breaks free from the expected social and moral boundaries and is against the law in Estonia.

Many evenings have been spent here at the leatherworks, sometimes talking, other times simply smiling. Yes, his Lordship and I have together reached the heights of ecstasy in a truly old fashioned way. It was all good clean fun, no pornography or sex aids were necessary, just a cow, preferably dead and a sturdy bar of saddle soap. Family entertainment really.

Given the intimate nature of my association with this fine upstanding fellow, I was appalled to learn that the Countess intends to sue him for defamation of character.

In recent years I have had scant contact with Lord Beauderriere as he now spends his time with the rich and famous. However, I have had the misfortune to have become acquainted with the Countess, which fills me with regret.

Following the untimely and somewhat comical death of her husband, the Countess sought refuge in England. Often in times of trouble and trauma, she returned to these shores. In the 1970's, when her corns were playing her up rotten, she spent a week recuperating in Blackpool. Then in the 1982 she fled Rome and travelled incognito to Ipswich after a liposuction experience that went tragically wrong. When she was widowed, she came to Buckinghamshire.

Her arrival went virtually unnoticed, despite the fact that she made one of her famous entrances. Lost and alone with no shoulder to cry on she found her way, by chance, to the door of the leatherworks.

I invited her in and we discovered a mutual friend in Lord Beauderriere. We chatted and drank wine, the rest is a blur. I awoke the following day lying on a floor slippery with saddle soap. I found the Countess, unconscious and spread-eagled on the cutting table. She was wearing nothing but a studded dog collar and a self-satisfied smile. Only a totally depraved harlot of raunchy demeanour could have driven me to such depravity, and she was it.

Since then I have prayed to God every night to forgive me. I have now returned to my innocent ways and have vowed never to fuck anything that moves ever again. His Lordship once told me that some old cow would get me into trouble one day, we never thought it would be the Countess.

I would like to stand up and be counted as one of Lord Beauderriere's staunchest friends. I swear that I am prepared to go down on my knees to express my absolute and unfailing support for him. I am also happy to assume that position during other activities, if the price is right.

Yours sincerely
Stanley Wimbles

The British Embassy
Government Square
La Santiado
Calamari

Mr Jeremiah Hanns
Hanns, Neece & Boompadasey
10307 Extortion House
Legal Lane
London W1

Dear Mr Hanns

It has come to my attention that there is some controversy over the proposed biography of the Countess de Verruca by Lord Beauderriere. His Lordship is a close, personal friend of mine and I know for a fact that anything he says is the paramount truth.

I would like to compound this by quoting two entries from a diary left here by his Lordship's father when he was Ambassador .

August 23 The Embassy: Weather hot, no rain yet. Held another reception last night for the President of Calamari and his wife, Mrs Bastado. That damn Verruca woman gate-crashed again.

I have informed the Embassy guards that if she tries to get in again they have my permission to shoot her on sight. When is it going to rain?

September 9 The Embassy: Weather hot, still no rain. I was awoken in the early hours of this morning by the sound of breaking glass.

The staff and I searched high and low for a broken window only to find that damn Verruca woman had broken in and smashed a bottle of my exquisite Chateau Parfait de Montenegro.

We found her on the study floor expertly lapping up the wine from amongst the broken glass. She was escorted to the roof of the Embassy and thrown off. We need rain and we need it NOW!!

I think the above goes a long way in vindicating his Lordship's writing and shows that there is a lot of truth in what he says. Lord Beauderriere is a frequent visitor to the island as he visits two of his businesses here. The Calamari Leather Works and the Pedro Valentino Saddle Soap Emporium.

Many a passer-by would see his Lordship burning the midnight oil to try to get those export orders out. They would hear him moaning as they pass, no doubt upset at the loss of any, although some bitter-minded people swear that he was moaning with lust, they have said they have seen him laying full length on a leather Chesterfield, stroking the arms of the sofa, smoking a cigarette and whispering "Was it alright for you?"

I know nothing of this, although I must add that I have seen him looking at my leather bound volumes of the History of Calamari with more than a wistful look in his eyes, but I am sure this is just his love of history.

Yours sincerely
Sir Herbert Titt
British Ambassador to Calamari

And then the Law stepped in!

THE CALAMARI COURTS OF JUSTICE
Parliament Square La Santiado Calamari

The plaintiff and defendant are called before
His Excellency Judge Juan Carlos Bastado
President for Life of The Republic of Calamari

Court of Calamari Plaintiff Dissertation

*Complaint No:*1784354

Name of Plaintiff: Countess de la Verucca
Name of Defendant: Lord Beauderriere

Complaint:

The Complaint has been issued by the Countess de la Verucca to impede the issuance of the Lord Beauderriere' imminent dissertation of the Countess in which it is postulated that good name of the Countess would be libelled. The Countess also brings this complaint because Lord Beauderriere has been abusive and vituperative of the Countess in public places and that notwithstanding letters from herself and her legal advisors, this has not ceased.
The Countess now wishes Lord Beauderriere to publicly recant the aforementioned calumny and denigration in the Court of Calamari where both the Countess de la Verucca and the Lord Beauderriere have residences and businesses and are so deemed residents of Calamari and subject to its laws.

Signed: Pablo Bastado
Court Secretary

And support from the Law!

**La Santiado Police Force
The Guardhouse Government Square
Santiado
Island of Calamari**

Dear Meester Hanns

Hullo, itsa me, Migual Bastado, Police Chief, big man in Calamari no? You willa probly heerd by now of the fantastico new book that isa bin writ by my good fren da Lord Beauderriere , grate personal fren, he comma ere alla tarm.

I fink itsa bout time that summerone put up the finger an probed da Countess as she assa bin nuffin but a pain ina my harse for a long tarm cummin now. She causes da trubble alla der tarm, wiv'r drinkin an he afondlin of my officers whena dey incastrate her.

She try alla tarm to pretend to be aal sweetness and lightenin, but no, she bloody cow she is and I have told her that she is person au gratin on this island and good riding to her.

His Lordship is rite in ever fing he say abart her. His Lordship is a hombre who is always upright and rigid like all British knobs and I willa have nuffink sed abart im.

Yours
Miguel Bastardo

And some with revelations!

REV. ARCHIBALD QUEER
St Wayne & St Sharon Church
Beauderriere Berkshire CH3 6RD

Contessa De Verruca
La Spinetta
Santa Maria Boulevard
Monaco

Madam

I was astonished when I learnt of the acrimonious malediction you have unleashed at Lord Beauderriere regarding his imminent thesis of yourself. Lord Beauderriere has, since early childhood, been a member of this congregation and if I could have a pound for every time I have seen him sitting in the family pew I would have a...pound.

As a young man he was a member of the church choir and was no different from the other boys save for the leather trim on his cassock. Many an evening was spent in quiet conversation with the young lord discussing world and local affairs, drinking tea and trying on leather miniskirts.

I am sure that whatever his lordship has said about you can only be the truth, so stop whinging you drunken old bat and bask in the reflected glory.

Yours faithfully
Rev. A Queer

Finally a letter from someone who was part of his life for many years.

GABRIELLE MOTHERSUBSTITUTE
Beauderriere Meadows
Beauderriere Hall Estate
Beauderriere City Berkshire

Mr Rodney Twinge
Twinge, Minge Cringe & Binge Solicitors

Dear Mr Twinge

I have heard on the old nanny grapevine that my dear boy, known to you as Lord Beauderriere, has been receiving nasty words from a lot of naughty people, this must stop now or no jam for tea.

How well I remember the first time I set eyes on the young Lord, I knew he was destined for great things. He would often leave the night nursery, run to my room, and get into bed with me. Oh what fun we would have, I would tickle him and he would have me sent down to the dungeon for a week, he knew that his status was well above mine even at that young age.

If ever the young Lord was late for dinner, he could always be found in the stable block playing with the tackle, both the horses and his own. I will not tolerate any further aspersions cast upon my dear boy, he looks after me very well and has given me a cottage on the estate for my retirement years and it only costs me £750 per week, oh generous boy.

Yours Gabrielle Mothersubstitute.

And the letter that halted the Countess's case and caused her to go into hiding!

Dobsons Peerage International
1 Burkes Street London W1 Tel: 002025547

The Countess de Verucca?
La Spinetta
Santa Maria Boulevard
Monaco

Dear Madam

I am writing following the recent publicity regarding the forthcoming biography of you by the eminent writer the Lord Beauderriere. On checking our extensive records to furnish tabloids with a potted history of you lineage, I have come across a problem that you may be able to assist me with.

According to our records, the title Countess de Verucca ceases following the death of Victoria, Countess de Verucca in a nasty Mixmaster Foodmixer accident in 1966. The Countess had no issue as the last Count was rendered impotent at the sight of his wife on their wedding night. I would therefore like you to forward to me details and incontestable proof of your right to the style and dignity of the aforementioned title.

Perhaps you can also assist me as to the whereabouts of the maid of the late Countess, Mildred Shufflebottom. Miss Shufflebottom disappeared on the night of the Foodmixer 'accident' with all the Countess's jewellery and designer clothes. This information would be gratefully received by the police forces of all the civilized world and America.

I look forward to hearing from you in the very near future.

Yours faithfully
Clarence Fink
Senior Researcher

I do not know the outcome of the above fiasco and quite frankly I do not care.

For a week or two, The Countess de Verruca was Clackhorne's Magazines In-House ~~Wino~~, sorry, Wine Expert. She didn't last long due to her continual drunkenness and the garbled audio cassettes she send in. She sent in one for a Hollywood Interview, it is a mish-mash of booze and her inability to remember what language she should be talking. It is disastrous, but very funny. Here it is!

Hollywood Interviews

Each Month one of our Columnists will interview a famous Hollywood Star. This month the **Countess de Verruca** talks to:

1930's Heartthrob Quentin Harcourt. Famous for such films as: The Lady Likes It, The Lady and The Gaucho and the

controversial The Lady Boy. Now 99 years old Quentin now lives in retirement at the Bel-Air Home for Retired Actors.

Countess: Duis autem Quentin, vel eum iriure dolor in The Lady Likes It, hendrerit in critics vulputate esse load of bollocks consequat, vel illum dolore eu feugiat nulla act like a wardrobe facilisis eros et accumsan et hendrerit in vulputate velit esse ought to give up acting molestie consequat?

Quentin: Zzzzzzzzz.

Countess: Wake Up! Duis autem vel eum iriure dolor in hendrerit before the pubs shut. In The Lady and the Gaucho vulputate esse consequat, vel illum kept falling off the horse. Esse leading lady Dolores Del Santiago eu feugiat shagged her nulla facilisis eros et accumsan nothing but a lecher et hendrerit the horse as well in vulputate velit esse molestie consequat prison sentence?

Quentin: Zzzzzzzzz. What, who's there? Zzzzzzzzz.

Countess: Duis autem vel eum iriure dolor in The Lady Boy hendrerit in vulputate esse consequat, got a lot of practice for the part in Bangkok. Vel illum dolore eu feugiat nulla facilisis escaped the police eros et accumsan et cannot return to Thailand hendrerit in vulputate nothing but a raving poof velit esse molestie consequat. Vel illum null aiusto odio?

Quentin: Zzzzzzzzz. Snuffle! Oh, hello my dear, do you know me? I used to be a famous actor. Are you my mother?

Countess: Facilisis lush eros et accumsan et fucking senile old idiot. Hendrerit in vulputate velit esse molestie anything that moved consequat. Nulla facilisis eros et accumsan et hendrerit in vulputate pissing off down the pub velit esse molestie consequat. Vel illum.

Two days after the interview, Quentin Harcourt passed away.

The Countess said this in memoriam. Facilisis lush eros et accumsan should have died long ago. Et velit esse molestie and putting his hand up my dress. Hendrerit in vulputate velit esse molestie consequat. nulla facilisis eros et accumsan et hendrerit in vulputate velit esse won't be able to close the coffin lid molestie consequat. Vel wanker!

Chapter Thirty Six
The Beauderriere Extended Family

Doctor Bogdan Beauderrierovitch

Dr. Beauderrierovitch is an Eastern European Monosyllabic Health Guru. He obtained his medical qualification from a shady character in a back street in Budapest. He is descended from the Beauderriere who fought at Waterloo. Captured by the Russians after that magnificent and stupid charge, he married a local Russian aristocrat and fathered an East European arms of the family.

All too aware that medical jargon and detailed diagnoses can worry patients, Dr. Beauderrierovitch, an Iron Maiden fan, set up the first on-line Medical Response Unit. Since then he had longed to appear on the Parkinson show and been asked to judge several pub quizzes in Birmingham.

Dr. Beauderrierovitch speaks very little English. Here is a selection of his early telephone consultations.

Doctor Beauderrierovitch, It hurts when I do this, What is your advice, should I stop doing it?

Yes.

Doctor Beauderrierovitch, I don't trust you even though you are a Doctor, is there something wrong with me?

Yes.

Doctor Beauderrierovitch, You may recall that some months ago I visited your squalid medical facilities in Harley Street, Pinner. I was, at the time, suffering from a suspected throat infection.

I have since deduced that the object your popped in my mouth was not a tongue depressor. Although I dutifully said 'agghh' at the time, as requested, I have since suffered nightmares and have been unable to eat sausages without gagging. Am I normal?

Yes.

Doctor Beauderrierovitch, You may recall that we spent some time together in a Turkish prison. I was suspected of drug smuggling (I was innocent of course) and you, if my memory serves me correctly, were accused (wrongfully I'm sure) of medical malpractice, fraud. And intention to perform major surgery with a rusty old Stanley knife blade
    I do vividly remember you telling me that you had no official medical training, (didn't you tell me you were a joss-stick salesman?) and that you planned, upon release, to go to England and set yourself up as a Doctor and 'con the thicko gits over there!'
    Sometimes I wonder if I dreamt all that. I always remember your kindness to me when I had a sore throat. Have I imaging all this?

Yes.

Doctor Beauderrierovitch, You may recall that I once consulted you about a nasty bolus on my sernedial pouch. You, very wisely suggested that light pressure to the epiglottis with a tongue depressor should do the trick. Since then my bolus has miraculously disappeared and I've had a sex change and have started my own market gardening business. Is there anyway I can thank you?

YES!

Doctor Beauderrierovitch, I am rather nervous of Doctors, am I being irrational?

Yes.

Doctor Beauderrierovitch, When I consulted you about an ear, nose and throat problem you told me to strip off. My husband has since found out and says your behaviour was unethical. He has no medical experience and I wonder if he's being over cautious. Is he?

Yes.

Doctor Beauderrierovitch, I recently approached my GP about having an affair with me. He said it would be against his principles. Are all Doctors so cautious and correct?

NO!

Doctor Beauderrierovitch, I'm sure I once bought a packet of mango scented joss-sticks off you in the old souk in Cairo! Was it you? I'm not sure now. Is my memory totally mangled by the constant use of drugs?

Yes.

Doctor Beauderrierovitch, Thank you for taking so much trouble of my clitoral realignment therapy. You seemed so dedicated and attentive that I wanted to call and tell you so others potential patients know. My sister-in-law, Beryl, who is frigid, says that you are completely out of order and ought to be struck off. I think she's jealous, don't you?

Yes.

Doctor Beauderrierovitch, You know I said I would meet you behind the autoclave next week? Well, I can't now because I've got to take our budgie to be put down. Would Tuesdays be alright and could the venue be the surgical waste troughs?

Yes.

Please remember, Doctor Beauderrierovitch is not a gynaecologist, no matter what he says or how hard he pleads!

Doctor Beauderrierovitch, Have you ever had the funny feeling that you're being watched?

Yes!

Doctor Beauderrierovitch, When you've had that feeling that you're being watched do you thinks it's because you're actually being watched r do you think you are suffering from paranoia? I think you're paranoid...are you?

Yes!

Doctor Beauderrierovitch, I've been watching you!

Oh!

Doctor Beauderrierovitch, Still think you're paranoid?

No!

Doctor Beauderrierovitch, Would you please send back my x-rays? The lounge looks so bare without them. Can I expect them by return post?

No!

Doctor Beauderrierovitch, Are you really mono-syllabic or do you sometimes speak normally using multi-syllable words?

Yes and No.

Doctor Beauderrierovitch, My name is Rupert Nanesque and I'm thinking of becoming a ballet dancer, do you think I have the legs for it? I enclose a pair of my most recently worn tights for examination.

Left leg Yes, Right leg No.

Doctor Beauderrierovitch, I keep thinking people are Norwegian. Am I Norwegian…I mean normal?

No!

Doctor Beauderrierovitch, I'm a linguist, does it necessarily follow that I might be Bi-Lingual?

Yes.

Doctor Beauderrierovitch, I am a twenty year old young woman who, despite everybody saying I have the body of a Venus and that I'm stunningly beautiful, I need someone to confirm this medically. Would you be willing to examine every part of my body closely.

Oh My God!

Doctor Beauderrierovitch worked for a time as medical advisor to Clackhorne's Magazine and conducted a Hollywood Interview for them.

Hollywood Interviews

Each Month one of our Columnists will interview a famous Hollywood Star. This month **Dr. Beauderrierovitch** talks to:

Action Movie Hero; Harry Sneidmann. Harry is famous for such films as Total Carnage, Total Carnage II, III, IV, V, VI, and Total Carnage: The Return Of Carnage

Dr Beauderrierovitch: Well!

Harry Sneidmann: Yes, I very pleased to be here.

Dr Beauderrierovitch: Yes.

Harry Sneidmann about me? I suppose you want to know all

Dr. Beauderrierovitch: Yes.

Harry Sneidmann: Have you seen any of my movies?

Dr. Beauderrierovitch: No.

Harry Sneidmann: Oh!

Dr. Beauderrierovitch: Well!

Harry Sneidmann: I understand that you are not a gynaecologist.

Dr. Beauderrierovitch: No.

Harry Sneidmann: Well, I played a doctor once.

Dr. Beauderrierovitch: Oh!

Harry Sneidmann: Yes, in a disaster movie.

Dr. Beauderrierovitch: Oh!

Harry Sneidmann: I think I'll go now if you don't mind.

Dr. Beauderrierovitch: No.

Harry Sneidmann: Very nice meeting you.

Dr. Beauderrierovitch: Yes.

It was after that that the Doctor booked himself into a Rest Home for the Sexually Bewildered for a long stay!

I have reached the bottom of the pile of Beauderriere Papers and there are no more.

    I hope you have enjoyed this saunter through history and my mind and if anything regarding the Beauderrieres surfaces again, I will keep quiet about it and burn all the evidence.

THE END! Or is it? Yes, it is!

Made in the USA
Charleston, SC
05 June 2014